Llŷr Gwyn Lewis is a Welsh-language writer, poet and essayist. *Flowers of War* is a translation of his first prose work, *Rhyw Flodau Rhyfel* (Y Lolfa, 2014), which won the Creative Non-Fiction category in the 2015 Wales Book of the Year award. His poetry collection, *Storm ar Wyneb yr Haul* (*Storm on the Face of the Sun*) (Barddas, 2014), was shortlisted in the poetry category in the same year, and his volume of short stories, *Fabula* (Y Lolfa, 2017), was shortlisted for the fiction category in 2018. He was selected as one of the Ten New Voices from Europe for 2017, as part of the Literary Europe Live project led by Literature Across Frontiers. In 2019 he was one of five authors included in the online magazine *Words Without Borders*' Welsh-language issue. He lives in Cardiff with his partner and son.

Katie Gramich is a writer, translator and Emerita Professor at Cardiff University. She has previously translated works by Kate Roberts, R. S. Thomas, and D J Williams into English.

T0167787

Parthian, Cardigan SA43 1ED
www.parthianbooks.com
First published as *Rhyw Flodau Rhyfel* by Lolfa, Talybont
2014
© Llŷr Gwyn Lewis 2014
English translation © Katie Gramich 2021
All Rights Reserved
ISBN 978-1-912681-25-9
eISBN 978-1-913640-46 0
Cover design and typesetting by Syncopated Pandemonium
Printed and bound by 4Edge in the UK
Published with the financial support of the Welsh Books
Council.
The publisher would like to thank Katie Gramich for her
support and commitment enabling the translation of this
book.
British Library Cataloguing in Publication Data
A cataloguing record for this book is available from the
British Library.

FLOWERS
OF
WAR

LLŶR GWYN LEWIS

TRANSLATED BY KATIE GRAMICH

For Nain, and in memory of Taid

PART 1

JANUARY 2011

About the middle of January in the year 2011 a feeling of restlessness descended on me and gradually transformed itself into a strong desire to embark on a journey. In the days leading up to Christmas, as the days shortened, I would find myself for hours on end daydreaming at my desk about this or that distant place to which I might escape, not indeed to the white beach baking under a tropical sun that's emblematic of such escape for, if truth be told, I would have been equally happy to travel to a place where winters were veritable winters for a change, though actually it was reasonably cold at home that winter and snow had been in the offing for the first time for some years. By January, my desire was still present though the snow had melted away, and I discovered that my research did not progress with enough ease and rapidity to guard me from my daydreams. It was always quite difficult to return my life to order after the idleness and leisure of the holiday season, but this year things were considerably worse than usual because I was in a relationship which was painfully dragging itself to its end and there was an ever-present knot of tension in the pit of my stomach which prevented me from throwing myself into my work. I feared that I would descend into some slough of self-pity and came to feel that to up sticks and leave without saying a word to anyone would be a way of extricating myself from my predicament with a mere backward glance and a vulgar gesture but, of course, like many of these dreams which would overwhelm me from time to time, I stayed, meek and timorous, precisely where I was, persevering with my books, and attempting to ignore the gathering clouds outside my window that had by this time been spreading themselves over the mountains for many weeks.

I had one other possible means of escape, for I had been meditating upon and sketching out in my mind a novel that I had been wanting to write for some years. The seed of the book had been planted when, with the typical zeal of the idealistic and patriotic young student, I had read a number of volumes, both fictional and factual, which might be described as to some degree revolutionary or militant, even icono-clastic. As a result of this, I was spurred on to create a similar kind of story set in the city where I was studying at the time. I was conscious, of course, of the lack of a realistic background for such a story and equally of the absence of an urgent need for political activism; true, I had participated from time to time in various protests and minor rallies when the revolutionary spirit had made itself felt in me, before it subsided once more, but there was no real need for a proper revolution or an underground movement in contemporary Wales and indeed, I found myself, while attempting to write my novel, almost envying those who lived in some of the countries of the Middle East who had begun to rise up against their governments at the time in what was already being labelled 'the Arab Spring'.

Such a feeling was of course abhorrent, and yet it was one I had felt before when I watched war films such as *Hedd Wyn*, which would arouse in me a trace of envy despite my recognition of the horrors of battle for, after all, my generation of young people was bereft of any great cause, or any 'just war' for which to fight, nor was there any other means, in truth, of putting to the test our own mettle nor of being able to declare that we had, in some way or another, 'done our bit' when we were called upon to do so, nor had we even proven our stoicism by struggling under difficult conditions. As I say, I was completely aware of the absurd, indeed odious, nature of such feelings and yet I could do no other than feel them, and as I look back it may even be possible to suggest that the attempt to write the novel was an attempt to make amends for these feelings in some way, through creative channels, and because I was conscious of the absurd nature of the desire, I distanced it by setting the novel in an imagined future in some kind of parallel universe, and yet simultaneously I longed to bring various locations, experiences and characters alive in the mind of the reader.

My lamentable state of *ennui* was not, however, an ideal basis by any means for writing such a work of the imagination. I was also plagued by increasing doubts about the feasibility of the project I was engaged upon, including the impossibility of speaking for the whole population of the city, or indeed any single person living there, since I was not a native of the city, and above all else perhaps the realisation that I had no insight, experience, nor understanding of any kind of violence, conflict, nor revolutionary or terrorist activity, since I had not even been known as a belligerent person in my schooldays, and so the underpinning of the whole plot and the events of the story would be so far outside my own personal comprehension that I found myself overcome by a sort of impotence, or paralysis, which meant that I could neither turn to my research nor write the intended novel, nor even drag myself away from the screen in case a flash of inspiration came from somewhere, which would be likely to vanish as suddenly as it arrived.

One day to give myself a rest, I took advantage of the opportunity to call at my grandparents', something I liked to do as often as I could whenever I was at home in the north, not from a sense of filial duty, for they were by now advanced in age and increasingly dependent on help given by family and friends, but indeed on the contrary because I myself enjoyed their company a great deal, was able to relax with them and enjoyed listening to their stories, and I must confess, because Grandma was a pretty decent cook. Grandad and I would share a knowing smile, understanding each other perfectly, and then after the meal we would go through to the front room with a cup of tea to watch TV or to tell each other stories, and I often thought that I should be keeping some kind of record of these conversations, but whether on account of my own lethargy or a feeling that perhaps their seeing me reach for a writing pad or a recording device might make them feel embarrassed or shy or, worse still, give them too obvious an indication that they were getting old, I hadn't up to now dared to do so.

This afternoon, however, both of them, Grandad in particular, were quieter than usual, and so, after our excellent dinner of chicken, potatoes, vegetables and bread and butter, and after washing up, we settled with our cups of tea in the front room, and the TV held sway. After half an hour or so of antiques and news programmes, I decided to take my leave, but as I rose my grandfather asked me to wait a minute and so I sat down again. He got to his feet slowly and, without saying a word, disappeared into the study at the back of the house. I looked at my grandmother, seeking some kind of explanation, but she looked back at me and shrugged, and before long my grandfather returned clutching a dusty cardboard folder that was evidently falling to pieces but was kept together with several elastic bands. My grandfather sat down again with a groan, and began to take the elastic bands off the folder, rolling them on to his wrist for the time being. My grandmother had been waiting just as eagerly as I, but I saw a sense of realisation spread across her face now and she began to look rather anxious as my grandfather thumbed his way through small sheets of paper that were contained within a larger file, itself slipped inside a large envelope, and underneath this I could see a substantial notebook with a greenish-grey cover. My grandfather beckoned me over to him, and I obediently did as he asked.

I stood in front of him, as he sat there, and he suddenly seemed to me to be very small and fragile, though he had a stocky physique and I knew perfectly well that he had seen many a day of hard labour, much harder than anything I had ever encountered in my life, and it was hard for me to see him like this in his armchair looking so vulnerable. There was the smallest hint of a tear in his eye, and the corners of his mouth were turned down, as he said to me 'Take this', and he gave me the small package, and the folder which was now back in the grasp of the elastic bands which he had removed from his wrist, and there was a slight trace of urgency and appeal in his voice as he spoke. Later, outside the house, as I started the car and waved to the two of them standing there at the window to see me off, I began to realize the significance of what Grandad had given me. I knew that he was soon going into hospital for surgery and that he was, in his own quiet way, aware of the dangers and the possible complications which might affect a man of his age after such treatment. Neither he nor Grandma would ever admit anything of the sort to me, but I sensed that he was giving me the package for safekeeping, just in case, and I guessed also that he wanted me to go somewhere on his behalf, for, as I thought at the time, it was likely to be a place that I could reach but to which he himself was no longer able to travel.

Turning the thing over in my mind, I remembered, from the whispers and half-told stories of my childhood, that my grandfather's brother, John, had been killed in the Second World War, but more than that I had never bothered to enquire, and by the time I was old enough to have an interest in hearing the story, I had lost my childhood boldness and was too conscious of the fragile physical, if not mental or at least emotional, state of my grandparents to start questioning them too much. In the car on my way back from their house, however, I was longing to look inside the shabby package that lay on the passenger seat beside me and seemed to be daring me to pull over, turn the engine off and to investigate its contents there and then. But I could guess with some confidence that the contents had something to do with John, or rather 'my grandfather's brother' as it seemed more natural to refer to him, and with his untimely death, as I imagined, in Germany during the Second World War.

As I steered the car around a corner and up the steep hill to the main road, the orange street lights suddenly brought to mind a drunken night that I'd once had with my friend Cynon when we were both nineteen and on a journey around Europe for a few months; we had watched Brazil beat Australia on the big screen in the Olympiapark in Munich, and were making our way back to the train and then Cynon, wearing the slogan 'Cynon ♡ Deutsch' across his chest, twisted his ankle as we ran across a bridge but a friendly taxi driver helped me carry him from under a tree, where he had fallen asleep, to the car, and again helped us find the way to the hostel. That was the last time I had visited Germany, but that memory led me back considerably further too, for I recalled the trip we had made as a family to Oberammergau, just an hour's drive from Munich, but a lifetime separated the two places for me.

For Oberammergau had been a real Bavarian town, one which conformed quite closely with the picture of Germany I had in my mind from early childhood, a place nestled among gigantic mountains, snow-topped even in the summer, and pine trees, and rain pouring down all around us, and the buildings with their protuberant façades, their beautifully painted walls, and the ubiquitous cuckoo-clocks which, in their own unique way, absolutely refused to let anyone forget the ineluctable and regular passage of time. Another indication of the passage of time in Oberammergau was the passion play staged there every ten years and which was, in fact, at the centre of and a *raison d'être* for the life of the whole community, so much so that the gigantic theatre built specifically to stage the passion play dominated the town centre. Indeed, that was the very reason we ourselves had come here, in order to see this unique pageant which was performed every day for five months in ten-year intervals, and almost every inhabitant of the town (and only inhabitants of the town) were in one way or another involved in it. The first performance of the *Passionsspiele* had, apparently, taken place in 1634, depicting as it still did the story of Christ from the time when he arrived in Jerusalem up to his crucifixion and resurrection, and it continued to be repeated in fulfilment of a vow taken by the village's inhabitants that they would re-enact these events every ten years if they were saved from the plague which was at the time spreading through the whole of Europe. Even today I still remember Christ arriving at the open-air stage riding a real ass, a detail which enchanted the other children and myself. I also remember, hours later, during a dinner break in the vast drama, we had eaten our sandwiches near the back of the theatre in the hope of catching a glimpse of Caiaphas in his tall hat popping to the lavatory, and had then returned to the auditorium to see the dramatic climax and had seen that the stage was now full and the rain was beating down so that the actors were soaked to the skin, and Jesus was being raised to hang on the cross, and the audience all in tears.

The price that the people of Oberammergau had paid for their rescue was to re-live and recreate the exact moment of salvation again and again, to preserve it and perform it and prevent it from sinking into oblivion, indeed to create it anew time after time, and I tried to imagine my parents, twenty years before they had shared this tremendous experience with us, going to see the previous performance when they had been a young married couple, and wondered how different it would have been for them this time around. Some elements must have changed so much that they were unrecognisable; for one thing they had three children to drag around after them this time, but on the other hand some things must have stayed so identical as to unnerve them, as regular and ineluctable as the song of the cuckoo in its clock. Of course, these rituals are essential, the juxtaposition and parallelism of the unchanging constant with the terrifyingly different was indispensable to the processes of memory, because of the need to be able to compare different points in our own lives. The people of Oberammergau, in the same way, told the same old unchanging story over and over but through ever new faces and figures, in order to be able to remember.

Although I was eager to open the folder and discover its contents, and was fully intending to do so the minute I arrived home at the end of the day, when I crossed the threshold there was the smell of cooking coming from the kitchen, and supper was soon on the table, and so I put the folder away for safekeeping under my desk, and hurried down the stairs again. A few hours later, after I returned to my desk in the study, my curiosity had waned and I had the faintest of headaches after having taken half a glass of wine too many with the meal, and so I vowed to examine the folder, in order to do it justice, in the light of day, but of course by morning work beckoned and eventually the folder disappeared under a mountain of paper and files.

*

Some months later, when I was single again and with my twenty-fourth birthday fast approaching, I had arranged to go to Italy for a fortnight, making my way from the north down to Rome, and less than a week before I left for Verona I was watching a programme on television in which a scientist was trying to explain to viewers the concept of entropy, a phenomenon that was a consequence of the second law of thermodynamics. I shall not pretend to have followed the explanation in every detail, but I was entranced, indeed astonished, by the presenter's explanation in which he used the analogy of a sandcastle in the desert. If one touches and plays with a heap of sand, explained the scientist, that does not have much effect on its shape, structure, or its fundamental nature, because the grains are not arranged in a particularly orderly or ordered manner. 'But if we create order', he went on, 'by building a sandcastle' – and luckily, he had to hand the very implements needed to accomplish that task, and he built a splendid castle before our eyes – 'my slightest touch, or even the action of the desert wind, is going to be enough to seriously impair the structure of the castle, and in the end to destroy it.'

Of course he added then, as a kind of footnote, 'there is no extant law which states that the wind cannot take up these grains of sand and deposit them somewhere else, by chance as it were, in the form of a perfect castle, but that would be exceptionally unlikely,' he said, 'because the general tendency of the systems of the universe, according to the second law of thermodynamics, is that things move from order to chaos, that is, from low entropy (the sandcastle) to high entropy (the shapeless heap of sand grains).' This in itself was quite a revelation for me, and the fact that I had succeeded in following most of the discussion was also a source of some self-satisfaction, but then the presenter went on to explain, because the law states that entropy can move only in one direction, namely from low entropy to high entropy, this was the only law in the whole of the system of physical laws which makes it absolutely necessary that time can only flow in one direction. That is to say, if it is essential that entropy can travel only in one direction, that must also be true of time – it can only move forward, because travelling backwards would mean that entropy would have to go backwards as well.

It was impossible for me to take in such revelatory and completely new ideas all at once, and I was still turning them over in my mind when the train on which I was travelling all of a sudden, or so it seemed to me, escaped from the suburban-industrial greyness of the Veneto into the piercing blue of the lagoon of Venice. It had all been bubbling away at the back of my mind throughout that visit to Italy, and as I made my way through the crowds in Santa Lucia station, I was almost heedless of my baggage and documents, not being vigilant against thieves and vagabonds, an attitude that is far from characteristic of me when on my travels. Even after I had left my bags in the hotel I had managed to find right on the Grand Canal, I wandered the tangle of streets and small canals more or less in a dream, unsure what to do next or where to go, and yet having no urge to plan ahead or to decide on a destination to head towards, and again this in itself was quite uncharacteristic of me, particularly in a foreign country.

I was sufficiently alert, however, to notice the numerous shops selling glass artefacts that I came across often in the course of my wandering, and though I was somewhat jaundiced after seeing the tenth glass-blower demonstrating his craft in his shop window, reminding me for a moment of those women displaying themselves in their shop windows, against a backdrop of red curtains, in Amsterdam, there was a certain attractiveness in those shops that sold the valuable products of the islands of Murano and Burano, either glass or lace, to the hordes of tourists since they were, after all, more dignified enterprises than the shops selling souvenir tat or bric-a-brac lining both sides of the Rialto bridge that were in competition with them for customers. As I watched one of these glass-artisans at his work my mind suddenly cleared for the first time since I had arrived in the city. I realised, as I watched the reshot Murano glass cooling, and taking solid shape in the various forms and colours selected by the glass-blower, that it was of the scientist and his explanation of entropy that I had been half-thinking for some hours, and that a visual embodiment of that process was being displayed before my eyes around every corner. I was reminded of that uneasy feeling that overwhelms one at times, when one comes across some technical, scientific term or even some quite common term, that one had lived one's life up to now without hearing at all, having once heard it for the first time and then hearing it regularly in a number of different locations and contexts. While the glass was in a fluid state the order within the chains of atoms would be chaotic, and so it was possible to mould and shape the material, within reason, into any shape one liked. Once it had cooled, the chains of atoms would be in order but, for that very reason, more fragile, and so that little ornament over there or this magnificent decanter, would only need to drop off the shelf or to be nudged by a nervous elbow in the narrow shop, for the objects to be reduced to broken splinters, with no possibility of being restored to their former shapes once more, and even though the glass-blower had, in his own way worked against entropy by creating order out of chaos, in the end it would be chaos which won the day and there would be no hope of creating order once more.

I decided not to rest and take a bite to eat and a drop to drink until I was thoroughly exhausted, my feet and legs aching and refusing to carry me any further. I sat down at last in a closed courtyard which was a mere stone's throw from the hubbub of the Rialto and yet was utterly still and silent. In one corner was an unprepossessing bar where I ordered a plate of cichetti and a large glass of dark Refosco, which had a bitter taste that complemented the morsels of bread and meat perfectly. Though my feet ached, my mind was still active and taken up now by the charm of the city. By the time I had finished my second glass, the mental wandering had turned to a laborious trudge, and my thoughts focused on the different powers that had affected, and which continued to affect, such a unique city. In its noble, elegant, artistically painted buildings, as well as in the gondolas and gondoliers with their striped clothing and hats, the red and white poles, the numberless stone bridges, I could see that other little detail that forms a part of the second law of thermodynamics, namely that it was possible for entropy to remain unchanging too, as well as to increase.

This was a city frozen in time, refusing stubbornly to change in any way. And yet at the same time I could hear the lapping of the waters against the canal walls down the alley, and I knew that the city was simply trying to deny the truth, and to conceal the inevitable, by refusing to allow any further development or new buildings, or in its dependence on the cheap souvenir shops for its income, and yes, I had seen the cracks in the red plaster on the walls of the Frari church where I had gone to see the famous painting by Titian of the Ascension of the Virgin, and yes, I had seen the wooden duckboards piled on top of each other along the walls in the shadow of St Mark's cathedral and the Doge's Palace, ready for when the floods came again with a little more force, and with even more certainty than the last time, to flood the square, and I realised that it would be entropy and chaos which would reign triumphant here too in the end.

But I began to suspect secretly that this was precisely the reason that this city exerted such a strong pull on me, because it was one of those few, increasingly rare, places in which time, if not exactly frozen into stasis, yet felt as if it were passing more slowly than anywhere else, and that there was more substance, more value somehow, in each second that passed in a place like this as a result of that arresting of time's flow. This sandcastle was stubbornly standing its ground, retaining each minute grain of sand, and one might almost, almost believe it possible to add a grain or two to each building, each plaster cornice, to command the flood to turn back and return once more to the sea, in essence, to turn back the flow of time itself. In Venice, one might imagine that one was at that critical point at which time stopped moving forwards and was about to begin to turn back, like standing on a beach at the very second when the high tide was about to ebb, or like pausing a video just as a ball has reached its highest point before falling back once more to the ground. This feeling of lightness, or rather of weightlessness stayed with me as I sat on the steps before Saint Mark's Square which led down to the open water where the canal opened into the lagoon, watching the gondolas getting dimmer in the twilight, and above them the great dome of San Giorgio Maggiore beginning to shimmer into light, and even later when I leapt onto the vaporetto and shoved my way to the front so that I could see how the boat ploughed its way through the water that was so black that it seemed like oil, adding to the sense of slowness, as the little lights above the palazzo walls hovered like insects over a swamp.

Two days later in Florence, however, the feeling began to wane and I was somewhat disappointed after having thought that the same enchantment that I had experienced in Venice was to be had in the other famous cities of Italy. In Florence there was none of that mist with a salty tang hanging over the city and the sun was just a little too fierce, and I found myself plodding from one ice-cream shop to the next, buying bottles of water and tasting the different flavours available in a vain attempt to prevent myself from getting too hot, but at about half past two I was overcome and was forced, like the Italians themselves, to take shelter indoors in the hotel, and there, having kicked off the bedsheets, I succumbed to the regular revolutions and the low humming of the fan and fell into a deep slumber. When I awoke the sun was already dipping below the horizon and my head was thumping, so I headed for the small fridge in the corner of my room and drank off half a bottle of water in one long swallow. I felt a little giddy and was obliged to sit down on the edge of the bed, but within a quarter of an hour or so I was feeling somewhat better and ready to escape from the confines of my room back into the city, and after a light supper of fish, bread, dry white wine and plenty of water in a back street bistro beyond the Duomo, I made my way in the darkness of night through the city streets, laid out in regular squares which connected up with one another and which were illuminated by some brilliant, white light. I fumbled my way through various open-air leather markets before finding myself, eventually, in the wide-open space of the Piazza della Signoria, where I enjoyed a cold beer on the terrace of one of the cafes as I watched the world go by. After a while, I saw a crowd gathering at the farther end of the piazza around the Loggia dei Lanzi, a strange building – or rather some kind of refuge – consisting of arches and carved Corinthian columns, which opened to the piazza, and was a square of three arches by three arches, containing a number of various Renaissance sculptures under its vaulted ceiling, and as I moved closer to the crowd I saw an orchestra of young people, with their conductor, gathering there under the arches, and preparing to play.

I bought a beer and stood around waiting for the orchestra to begin playing, and when the music started I was on the verge of tears, for the pieces they played were so sad and beautiful, managing to express a tragic, grand dignity bordering on the pathetic, and at the same time I recall now, listening to the music replaying in my head, that at least one of the violins, if not two or three of them, were the slightest bit out of tune, or at least were finding it difficult to reach the highest notes, and of course that was perfectly understandable with a youthful orchestra like this, and yet in truth, rather than impairing my enjoyment, that endowed the music with an additional element of beautiful melancholy, and in spite of myself, and though I wished to allow the music to wash over me in the moment, I found myself with my phone out filming the whole thing, turning around on the spot in order to obtain a panoramic film of the square, the grand façades and the square, threatening shadow of the Palazzo Vecchio presiding over the entire scene.

When I arrived home a little over a week later, I was glad that I had filmed this experience, because I now had the opportunity to make enquiries from friends who had more musical knowledge than myself, about what exactly the pieces were and who had composed them, and I also busied myself with playing with special effects on the video so that I turned it into a grainy, black and white movie which had a tendency to jump and flicker from time to time, and that effect, in combination with the buildings, that strange bright white light, and the threatening presence of the Palazzo Vecchio above it all, inevitably reminded me of an old film clip from the Second World War. I discovered afterwards, in trying to reverse this effect, that it was impossible to do so, and that the original film had been lost, so that I can't bear to watch the short black and white clips any more because of their tendency to unsettle me, like documents from some lost period of my life, a tendency exacerbated by the fact that I never to this day succeeded in finding anyone able to recognize or name the film's music or its composer, so that I began to question whether I ever had this experience at all, or whether it had all been a dream brought on by the relentless midday sun, the afternoon nap and the rapture of the lovely young evening.

By the time I reached Rome, I had begun to long quite urgently to return home, and wished to see the two days that remained of my trip disappear, so I did not do much in the great city, except to take a few brief turns around the Forum and to spend the rest of the time eating and drinking wine in the many tourist cafes clustered in the shadow of the Coliseum.

As I walked around the Forum, the political and commercial centre of Rome from the early days of the Republic up to the height of the Empire's power, my mind turned once more to entropy, that strange phenomenon that had dominated my thoughts throughout my sojourn in Venice, and I remembered the rule about the impossibility of reversing the operation of entropy, that is, the impossibility to move from high entropy to low entropy, from chaos back to order, and I reflected that the only beings in the universe, as far as I was aware, who attempted to rebel against this law were people, as manifested in their invention of basic objects like the fridge, or by building, through bringing together atoms of sand to create glass, stones, walls, and then creating out of these more structures, columns, gigantic buildings like the ones right here in the Forum. As I leafed through my tourist guide in the various temples and marketplaces, I found another example when I saw a depiction of the Forum as it had been a little over a hundred years ago, when it had been full of soil, and it was possible to see only the tips of the arches and the columns rising out of the earth, and when it was being used as a cattle market, and I learnt then that the Romans had taken upon themselves the task of excavating these buildings and revealing them, work that began at the turn of the nineteenth century but which was not completed until the twentieth, and thus the place was transformed from chaos into order.

I was also aware, however, from reading the various signs dotted about the site warning one not to climb on the walls or touch the doors, in case they turned to dust beneath our feet or in our hands, that the Forum, since it had been uncovered and exposed to the elements, was yet again slowly going to rack and ruin and returning again to chaos, and that the second law of thermodynamics therefore still held sway, despite all the efforts made to resist it. I was on the brink of wishing that the archaeologists of the nineteenth century had let the entire Forum lie in peace, untouched beneath the earth, because I had been walking around the place for quite some time with my guidebook in my hand, trying to match up what I could see in the various diagrams and maps, the basilicas and temples, the gardens and the marketplaces, the grand arches with their fine decoration, with what I could actually see in front of me.

But it was scorching hot and the ruinous state of all these places meant that there was no shade to be found anywhere, and although I refilled my bottle more than once at the several taps which dispensed tepid water, and though I took many breaks, I grew increasingly weary and ill-tempered, partly, I think, looking back on it now, because of my sense of frustration that I failed utterly to link up any of these locations with their former appearance, according to the diagrams in the guidebook. That is to say, I could trace the shape of the Basilica Aemilia by the way in which its foundations were laid out at ground level, and I experienced a certain thrill in finding a few denarii which had melted into the ground when the building was burnt down in AD 410. I could see the outline of the temple of Romulus lurking behind the nave of the church which it had been turned into later, and I could see where Vespasian's temple had stood on account of the three remaining columns at one of its corners which still thrust themselves vigorously up into the air. But I couldn't for the life of me imagine the place exactly as it had once been, as the ancient Romans had seen and experienced it, and that was probably on account of the many different strata of history that by now lay thick upon it.

So, after wandering fairly aimlessly past the Coliseum, I stopped at a little cafe for an espresso and a *cornetto* pastry before continuing my way down the Via di San Giovanni in Laterano, and I came across a heavy wooden door that was closed and which informed me that this was the entrance to the Basilica of San Clemente and that it would cost me three Euros to visit the archaeological excavations underneath the church. The church I stepped into in any other city, I'm sure, would have been a source of pride and publicity and a focus of the tourist industry, but in this city it was just one of many quite similar churches, a place to pause for a while on one's way from the Coliseum to San Giovanni in Laterano, a handsome building but not an exceptional one. It had been built in the twelfth century, apparently, and its most noteworthy features were the somewhat down-at-heel cloister in the front where grass grew between the cracks in the tiles, and above all else perhaps the golden mosaic above the altar in the apse, displaying all manner of creatures, from sheep to griffons, surrounding a crucified Christ in the midst of a circle of saints and decorative acanthus leaves.

The current Pope had written an article about this mosaic, and the booklet was for sale in the shop in one of the chapels to the right of the nave, but I didn't succumb to the temptation to buy it, instead paying my three Euros and venturing down the broad stairs where I was greeted immediately by the cold smell of the soil, as if I were already deep in the bowels of the earth. This church, erected in the fourth century, and on top of which the current church was built, was quite a cavernous space. Perhaps it was the low ceiling that created the impression that the body of this church, filled with columns in intermittent rows, was broader than that of the building above it. I spent considerable time in the portico at the entrance, and the first thing that struck me was the faces carved upon the walls, which still thrust themselves forward with remarkable clarity, except that the faces themselves, features such as the eyes, noses, and mouths, had been blunted and smoothed out, and I thought as I looked at them how ironic it was that we were so eager, so desirous to remember and to live our past lives, and yet we were so incapable of doing so properly because our memories were so bitty, so incomplete, so fragmentary, like these faces which had been eroded away.

In this narthex there were several colourful frescoes which had survived from the end of the ninth century and the beginning of the tenth, frescoes that portrayed different episodes in the life of the early Popes, none other than Clemente himself. Here too, placed on a kind of axle, was a gravestone, and if one turned it it was possible to see that there was a Christian inscription on one side, and on the other a 'Pagan' memorial, as the information panel put it; both were in Latin, as anyone who turned this stone on its axis could see, and in so doing one could as it were touch two worlds which had coexisted and overlapped each other, and yet the two were facing in completely different directions. I ventured into the main body of the underground church, illuminated by lightbulbs erected on poles, which shed a cold, bluish-white light around, and I came across one fresco that was more complete than the others and which demanded my attention for some reason.

This fresco struck me because of its colour and its detail; it depicted a chapter in the life of Saint Alexis of Rome, who, according to the information panel's version of the story, was brought up in a gentry family in the city, his father being a senator. He had been determined to devote himself to his faith, but to avoid bringing shame upon his family he agreed to an arranged marriage. The day after the wedding, with the bride's blessing, he fled to the town of Odessa in Syria, to live a life of extreme poverty as a hermit, consecrating his life to the service of God, and so he lived for years, it seems, without being recognised by anybody, not even the servants who were sent from his home, poor things, to Syria to look for him, until the Virgin Mary appeared before the people of Odessa and informed them of the sanctity of this pauper who was living in their midst. He then fled once more, full of shame, and he knew of nowhere else to go except back to Rome, where he sought shelter once again in his former home, where no-one recognised him, not even his parents or his wife, for his appearance had changed so completely. And so he lived for a good seventeen years, Alexis working for his own family among all the other servants, acting as a scripture teacher to the children and spending the rest of his time praying and fasting and living under the stairs, and I tried to think of what exactly could have happened to him, how he could have been transformed to such an extent that his own family didn't know him. Was there some indiscernible part of him, something that made Alexis Alexis, that had been left behind in his great haste to flee from Syria, perhaps? And why did he return to live amongst the very people who were most likely to recognize him? Was the attraction of home as invincibly strong as that, then, and how on earth did Alexis manage to keep the thing secret from his family for so long, indeed, going to the grave with his secret intact?

But there was, of course, one thing that he forgot. When he died, he had in his hand all his essays and stories, but the dead hand's grip upon them was so tight that it was necessary to call in the Pope himself to pull the papers out of his hand, which had stiffened into a claw on account of *rigor mortis*, I imagined, though it would be easy to suggest a more supernatural explanation of the thing, for it was only through the miraculous intervention of the Pope that these writings were retrieved, read, and thus his parents discovered that it had been their own son who had served them in such a godly manner for close on twenty years. The ensuing scene was depicted in this fresco: the grief felt by his family as his body was carried away, and the one figure that really caught my attention was the little, silent, background figure of the wife, standing framed by a window, shut in and separated from the chaos and tumult of the grieving multitude outside, and I was unable to make out any sign of emotion on her face, but I did feel at the same time, that in the midst of the busyness and movement of the picture, that she was looking from her position at the window directly out at me.

Above the main panel of the fresco there was a painting of God with a number of saints on each side of him, and the remarkable thing about it was that the upper part of the picture was nowhere to be seen because this representation of God had been decapitated, God having been sacrificed in order to lay the foundations of the church above. As I wandered afterwards through the aisles on either side of the main body of the church, peering into an alcove here and there and finding a spring that had run dry, I realised that I could nevertheless hear the sound of water running somewhere, and I followed that sound to the furthest corner of the church, to the left of the chancel, where I found stairs leading down yet another level.

I had come across one or two other visitors as I meandered through the columns, but as I descended these stairs I realized that I was now completely alone, and at the same time I noticed the thin red tiles set in a herringbone pattern underfoot which was still intact but was protruding from the earth here and there, as if reaching out to me from the first century AD. For it was from that century that this level dated, and I found myself now in a kind of hallway of decorated columns. On the wall on one side was an iron gate which barred the way to a narrower, darker chamber, a *triclinium* that was almost a cave and in its midst stood an ancient altar dedicated to the god Mithras with a carving of him facing out towards me, in the act of killing a bull; it was lit by one of those lamps which showed that on either side of the altar under the low ceiling and the apse and reaching around the side walls were two marble benches where the early worshippers of the Mithraic cult would, probably, have sat in order to partake of the ritualistic feast. Further down a narrow corridor on the right, which one couldn't go down, one caught a glimpse of another room closed off and dimly lit, which had once been used, according to the information panel, as a Mithraic school, whatever that might have been.

But as I returned to the triclinium, and went through the small entrance, I came to a narrow, constricted alleyway between two buildings, and I don't know why but that was more impressive to me, almost, than the Mithraic altar I had just seen. I stood there for a while looking at the earthen floor and at the ceiling which had once, I imagine, been a thin strip of blue sky, and then strode into the building on the other side of the alley, the house of a Roman alderman of the first century who, according to the information provided, had been one of the first in the city, if not the entire Empire, to experience a conversion to Christianity and who had therefore used his home as a refuge for others of the same persuasion, all this just a stone's throw from the Forum and under the very nose of the Emperor. Here again the thin red tiles led me in zigzag fashion through the rooms of the house, and the tiles on the walls, too, still bore traces of colour and pattern, and through it all was the vibrant sound of running water which came from I knew not where, not until I reached the last room, impossible to go further, and there, at the end of this room, there stood a kind of bench-like trough with a series of covers, one of which had been left open. I crossed the room and saw an illuminated hole in the wall from where a stream of cold, clear water ran into the trough and then disappeared beneath the covers. I stood there for some minutes before I remembered that I had a bottle of water in my pocket that was almost empty, and felt a temptation to fill it, but for some reason I stopped myself. Nevertheless, I felt that I had at last succeeded in pulling back the layers of time, almost like scratching off the scab from a wound, and all that was needed to produce that feeling, apparently, was the sight of this clean running water still taking its unchanging course through the old pipe.

My thoughts were rudely interrupted by a noisy Roman-American who wanted to show 'Rome's best-kept secret' to two of his friends, and who took over the room in his own inimitable way, so it was in a sort of dream that I climbed back up the stairs, through the levels, noticing on my way a fragmentary fresco of the Last Judgement, which included three rows of terrified people in close-up, and so when I emerged, at last, from the oppressive cold into the burning heat of the sun and raised my eyes to the sky, it was those faces that I saw seared on the back of my eyes like a photographic negative. I awoke next day, my last day in Rome, with my face all swollen, red, and itchy, and that fact exacerbated my feeling of dissatisfaction and annoyance since I had to fly home in that state, feeling exceptionally self-conscious. There was a strange coincidence about the timing of this quite severe allergic reaction, and I began to wonder if it had something to do with my visit the previous day to the church, temple and underground house, the cold and dampness of the air there, or the fact that I had dared to touch, lightly, one of the tiles in the Roman house with my fingertips as I passed through one of the doors. I began to regret that I had not drunk my fill of that running water because whatever its effect might have been, it could not have been worse than the ghastly apparition that looked back at me when I faced the mirror that morning, and who knew, perhaps it would have had a healing and rejuvenating effect upon me? I would never know now, but believing that a reaction to the damp, pagan air of the Mithraic temple was less discomfiting than the growing suspicion at the back of my mind that it was all a reaction to the red wine that I had drunk the previous evening, and that I had begun to develop some sort of an allergy to one of Mithras's distant cousins, Dionysus or Bacchus.

The day was grey and wet, the first rainy day I had experienced since arriving in Italy a fortnight ago, so it was with wet feet that I made my way to the hospital, but by the time I found the right department among the labyrinth of old Georgian buildings that had seen better days, had given my particulars and waited my turn, I realised that I would have to leave quite soon in order to catch my plane. I apologised hastily, therefore, pointed at my face and asked for *crema* in a nearby pharmacy, caught a taxi to the airport, and indeed I believe I would have been able to remain reasonably optimistic, facing my destiny if not with acceptance at least with stoicism, had it not been for the fact that, after paying the taxi driver 55 Euros and shouldering my rucksack, I realised that I had left my cap, a tweed cap I had bought in Ireland some years previously and of which I had grown particularly fond, on the seat of the taxi which had by now disappeared back into the maw of the great city, leaving me depressed and discontented. And this was the state in which I arrived home at the end of my travels.

*

In this mood I found myself late that night, completely exhausted after the journey and in sore need of rest, being drawn inexplicably despite myself, not towards bed in order to sleep as I knew I should, but rather towards the desk in the study, which was fairly uncluttered, since I had, more conscientiously than usual, finished most of my tasks on time and had tidied up in a rather self-satisfied way before I left for Italy. I don't know if it was because I was conscious that I had flown over Germany on the flight home, or on account of some advert I'd seen in the airport about cheap flights to Berlin, but I was reminded again of that folder, or perhaps indeed it had been all that thinking about the passage of time that had been prompted by the marvels of Italy, but in any case in the lamplight, without bothering to switch on the main light, I reached for the folder and opened it carefully, laying out its contents before me. The first thing I picked up, being the most striking, was the big greenish-grey book, eight inches by ten, with the title:

1939–1945
THE WAR DEAD OF
THE BRITISH COMMONWEALTH
AND EMPIRE

And then, in smaller print at the bottom, CEME-
TERIES IN SYRIA, TURKEY AND CYPRUS. In
the top left-hand corner these names appeared again,
followed by numbers, as follows:

SYRIA 1–3
TURKEY 1–4
CYPRUS 1–4

I was somewhat nonplussed by these inscriptions
since I had long been under the impression that my
grandfather's brother had been killed somewhere in
Europe, and though the two great wars were known
as World Wars, I shared the general belief that the
First World War had taken place mainly in Europe,
particularly along that more or less unmoving line
down from Belgium through France to Switzerland,
which tore the continent into two fairly neat blocks.
That belief also influenced my vague conception of
the Second World War, or at least it made me imagine
that anyone with some family or personal connection
to me would have been involved in the war in Europe,
which was far enough away not to be considered close
and yet not so far away for one to lose sight of events
and movements there. If the Second World War was
something that had happened to other people, people
of another generation, then for me it was almost as
if the conflict in Burma, Japan, and north Africa had
run its course in a different universe.

And yet, it now seemed that a blood relative of

mine had been part of the conflict in these far-flung places and had even, somehow or other, got himself killed in that conflict. I leafed through the pages and found, among the columns of names and numbers, diagrams and maps of the various cemeteries, and tables recording the various nationalities of the dead interred there. I closed the book once more, and then opened it at random, and found that it opened of itself at a particular page, and there, half way down the first of the two columns on the page, were two marks, made with a pink highlighter, beside one of the names and the details that followed:

Jones, Gnr. John Owen, 96—8. 60 Field Regt., Royal Artillery. 23rd June, 1941. Age 24. Son of John Morris Jones and Elizabeth Jane Jones, of Llangedwyn, Denbighshire. P. 44

and that final little detail referred, of course, to the place where John was buried. I turned therefore straight away to the diagram of the cemetery, and found the plot, quite far from the entrance, in a row which was one of two that encircled the central, much larger, plot where the dead from the First World War were laid. According to the foreword to this part of the book the cemetery was some five kilometres (three miles) outside Damascus, on the way to the airport, and it was possible to reach it easily by bus or taxi from the city. According to this 1959 guide there was ample good accommodation to be found in Damascus itself, and the cemetery was established in October 1918 when British troops entered the city, and found the Turkish hospitals overflowing with sick and injured casualties, but it was not until a few days later when there was an outbreak of cholera and flu in the city that, quite suddenly, it was necessary to find a place to bury 597 bodies. After the fighting in 1941, a number of bodies were moved from various smaller and more scattered locations to this spot, where they were buried in the area between the surrounding wall and the graves that were already there. Later, another row of graves was added to the west, and was called The Cypresses, a name that struck me as both appropriate and utterly inappropriate simultaneously. It would have been an ordinary kind of name for an old people's home in suburban England, somewhere like Rochdale or the Wirral, places, I thought, in which most of the people buried here could have spent the last years of their lives. For a moment the cruel and completely irrational thought struck me that they were actually better off in this place, a thought which sprang from a mixture of knowledge of how appalling some old people's homes could be, though not all, and some kind of "They shall grow not old, as we that are left grow old" sentimentality that they had been struck down in the prime of life and they would never have to suffer the shame and pain of old age.

But my train of thought was interrupted when I remembered my grandparents contently ensconced in their swelteringly hot living room, and as I looked again at the booklet I was overwhelmed by a sense that I was interfering, poking my nose into something I knew nothing about and where I wasn't wanted, and I could do no more than cast a swift glance over the rest of the details that described the Stone of Remembrance at the farthest end of the cemetery, noting that the roof was made out of Roman tiles from Cyprus, and that the graves of the unknown dead bore the inscription

Their glory shall not be blotted out.

Through it all my mind was still reeling with the shock of reading two details in particular, namely John's age when he was killed, twenty-four, which was precisely my own age at that time, and the date, the twenty-first of June, or the Summer Solstice, which had but recently gone by when I was in Italy, and as a backdrop to all this, though I had never been to Syria, and I had only a diagram and the brief description of the cemetery to go on, I nevertheless could conjure up a remarkably clear image of it in my mind's eye.

Perhaps, indeed, the cemetery was all too familiar, at least in my mind, similar to the only war cemeteries I had ever visited, namely those dedicated to the dead of the First World War in the Ypres region of Belgium; these were cemeteries I had actually visited more than once, more often than most people and more often than was quite sensible for a nineteen-year-old, which is the age I had been when I last visited the area, accompanied by my friend, Cynon. That time, I was determined to show him Hedd Wyn's grave in the Artillery Wood graveyard, for I had myself experienced there a kind of thrill when I had been there more than once with my parents, a macabre thrill perhaps but a thrill nevertheless.

In the photograph albums at home there were a number of pictures of us at different times kneeling before this grave or standing behind it, and we had I expect signed our names in the visitors' book at least four times over the years. I can't be certain what drew us as a family back there time after time, nor why we revisited the Cafe Hagebosch not far from the cemetery, which had been used as a field hospital during the war and where Ellis Humphrey Evans had been carried from Pilkem Ridge, on the battleground of Passchendaele, with a piece of shrapnel lodged in his back, where he was given morphine, since there was no hope of recovery, and where he died, on the last day of July, 1917. There are pictures of me there too, standing in front of the café, since it wasn't possible to go or even look inside, for it seemed, in that characteristically Franco-Belgian way, asleep or to have been slumbering for years in the fierce heat of the afternoon sun, while we were the only fools in the place, loitering about the slate plaque that had been set into the red brick wall and which told Hedd Wyn's story and displayed his picture, though it didn't resemble him much, and an image of the Black Chair. This plaque has served as a kind of family height-measuring chart, for my own growth can be seen according to how far back my mother or father had to stand in order to fit both myself and the plaque into the picture. By the time I'm about twelve, my teeth too big for my face, I'm wearing a huge pair of spectacles and standing beside the plaque which is at shoulder height and the picture is much more of a close-up than the others, and you can see that strange kind of smile that I tended to put on my face in that kind of situation, as if I couldn't quite decide, perhaps because the tragic nature of the story had dawned on me for the first time and was in conflict with that former macabre thrill, whether I should smile or frown or weep copious tears, and so in the end adopted a strange expression which looked as if I were blinded by the sunlight.

That last time, we had to book an official trip with a guide and a minibus, since we had no car and it had always been my father who had found the place thanks to detailed instructions he had got from a local historian, but when Cynon and I asked whether we could perhaps take a short detour to see the graveyard and cafe, the guide knew immediately the place we wanted to reach, and the small group of other visitors were perfectly happy to go there too. So after seeing the bunker where John McRae had written his poem about Flanders Fields we got the opportunity to go to our small corner of a foreign field that is forever Wales.

Looking at the visitors' book, it was clear that a number of other Welsh people had felt, like us, a queer sense of ownership of that graveyard, and yet it was unsettling to be there without my family and with a group of strangers, listening to this man who was, after all, not "one of us", though he was remarkably knowledgeable, intelligent and sensitive, telling us the story of Hedd Wyn, every tiny detail of which I already knew, but he was informing the other tourists, and adding technical details such as the movements of the battalion, the timing of the battle, and something I had never thought about before, namely what happened in the battle after Hedd Wyn fell, quite early on in the conflict apparently and afterwards the battalion had taken Pilkem Ridge and had advanced towards the place known as Iron Cross, all of which made the familiar story sound somewhat strange.

As he finished his narrative he startled us by turning suddenly to the two of us and asking us whether we had anything to add, or any lines to recite. Cynon shook his head at once, of course, refusing to say a word but the other visitors looked at me so expectantly and hopefully that I felt a kind of duty to satisfy them, and in those circumstances I found myself racking my brains to remember the words of Hedd Wyn's poem 'War' and reciting it beside the grave, rather tentatively at first but by the last verse, unexpectedly, overcome with emotion. It was only when Hedd Wyn's harps were hung on the willows and the young men's shouts disappeared into silence that I got control of myself and realised fully where I was. I felt a bit like a monkey who has just been egged on to perform amidst the murmurs of approval as the group spread out among the rows of graves before returning to the minibus, their comments on Welsh, 'lovely language, so poetic', until Cynon turned to me and admitted, in a tremulous voice, that he had felt a lump in his throat and a tear on his cheek and that he hadn't, until that moment, fully understood the words and their significance.

The previous day Cynon had refused to go with me to hear the Last Post at the Menin Gate because there was an important football game on in the World Cup, and so I had made my way over by myself, feeling strangely lonely since of course I was used to being there with my family, and as I listened to the notes reverberating under the arches of the gate, as if the thousands of names inscribed there were sending out their echo to us through the decades, I was uncertain what exactly I was commemorating, whether it was all these soldiers together, or that single unknown soldier, or perhaps my own childhood. Now, though, Cynon was fully in sympathy with the journey, and when the minibus stopped at the next place, namely Tyne Cot cemetery, near Zonnebeke, the biggest war cemetery in the world, he was the first to get out of the bus. I watched him from afar in his shorts, sandals, and sunglasses, making his way over the neat, short grass, between the rows of immaculate white gravestones, and pausing before almost every one of the stones, but by the time he reached the third row I noticed that he had slowed down considerably, and by the time I caught up with him I found him standing, gazing down at a grave which had no specific name upon it but rather that famous phrase by Kipling

A Soldier of the Great War
Known Unto God

The guide had already explained to us how Kipling had urged his son, John, with his usual jingoistic enthusiasm, to join the army, and that this son, barely two days after he was sent to the front, had been killed, and the last description of him which was of his stumbling blindly through the mud, screaming in pain after a piece of shrapnel from an explosion had torn his face to shreds, contrasted appallingly with the glorious image that had probably been in Kipling's mind as he had had a quiet word in the ear of Lord Roberts to ensure that his son, who was iron-ically quite short-sighted, was allowed to enlist. John's body had never been found and identified for cer-tain, and as a result Kipling had asked for that stark and striking sentence inscribed on his gravestone, and the guide explained how that sentence had then been adopted as a formula to be used on every grave where an unknown dead soldier lay and that it could be adapted according to what was known about the poor lad, for instance

An Australian Soldier of the Great War
Known Unto God

'It's not that,' Cynon murmured, when I suggested to him, as a way of getting him to move on instead of standing there as if mesmerised above the grave, that this poor lad had been given the same kind of burial and service as every other soldier, 'it's just that there's so many of them'. It was true; I learned from reading the information booklet about the cemetery in the museum at Cloth Hall in Ypres later, that 8,367 of the total of 11,954 dead soldiers buried there were unknown, and so it didn't surprise me that Cynon, moving from one grave to the next along the rows in this way, and finding grave after grave marked with the same sentence and variations on it, felt the whole thing weighing down upon him, or rather as if it grabbed hold more and more tightly of his legs, until he was simply unable to move on, completely overwhelmed by a lack of comprehension, an inability to grasp what he was seeing in front of him, what he was experiencing, that it was all too much, too much for him to be able to consign it all to memory.

In a way, it was easier to meander later on towards the huge wall at the furthest end of the cemetery that was built when it was found that the Menin Gate wasn't big enough for all the names of the soldiers who were missing but whose bodies were never found to be inscribed there. 'Perhaps some of these names on the wall here correspond with the bodies in the graves over there', I said. 'Perhaps', said Cynon, doubtfully, but somehow the wall with the list of names was more palpable for him; he was able to grasp it more readily and he spent quite some time searching through this very long list for a name that was similar to his own. I did the same, and found the inscription

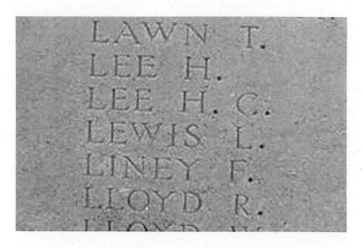

If there's one thing that still stays in my mind from Tyne Cot cemetery it's that one name, something that was in its distance and singularity, perfectly at one with our lives and our way of living; we were overwhelmed and yet we continued to search, among the heaps and lists and objects and names and things, for something to get hold of and to identify with, something recognizable, familiar. In the same way, it had been easier for me in some strange way the night before to feel the weight of the tall columns of name after name after name above me on the walls of the

Menin Gate than it had been to concentrate on the flame of that one unknown soldier in the middle at ground level, and the disturbing notes of the bugle. Having the map, with its straight lines and its neat numbers, in front of me, and knowing exactly where to put my finger on the map to identify the place where my grandfather's brother lay, gave me almost a feeling of satisfaction, and was considerably easier than reading the extraordinary details about the different inscriptions that were engraved on the walls there.

It's probable that this satisfaction I felt came from the fact that being able to put your finger on a map was a kind of embodiment, a way of transforming into a flesh-and-blood person a great-uncle whom I'd never known and about whom I'd heard only scraps of sentences, though that was certainly my own fault for not listening out for his name or his story, my ears not attuned to a sigh or a whisper at the end of a tale. However, I now had an easy and readily available method of getting to know this young man, whom I regarded rather oddly as a contemporary, through the little pile of letters, correspondence and other bits of paper that were included in the folder. But I hesitated for a long time before making a start, sitting passively at my desk, trying to think of other things to do and finding it easy to let myself get distracted by the TV, the radio or the internet, and it was only by switching off these machines completely, exerting considerable willpower, that I succeeded finally in dragging myself towards the folder, surprising myself by how reluctant I was to browse through the contents despite my desire to put a face and a voice and a personality to the skeleton of a name.

Once I'd plucked up courage at last, I reached for the folder and found that there were two bundles there, as well as the list of graves, one pile of papers held together by an elastic band, and another lesser pile stuck into a small envelope. My attention was immediately drawn to the letter on top of the bigger pile, which bore the letterhead, in green ink,

and a small picture of a quill pen and an incept in green beneath, and the date August 26th, 1936, informing my uncle John, with pleasure, that he had passed with honours the examination to be a Stationer's Assistant. Reading further, I saw that he had presented himself for the examination under the auspices of a Manchester bookseller, and I therefore realised that John, like Arthur, my grandfather's other brother, must have gone to live and work in

Manchester, and that he had been there when war broke out three years later. John must have been an able young man, then, and that impression was strengthened when I took the plunge and carefully extracted the contents of the small envelope, finding that it was held together by a Christmas card, with a picture of a gay holly wreath hanging on a door, as if it were inviting me to open that door and discover the lights and the celebrations and the joy within. However, the contents were nothing of the sort, and the two first letters that I encountered were ones whose covers looked too threateningly official, so I placed them to one side for the moment.

The next item in the pile was a small piece of folded grey paper, and I picked that up too, intending to move on, but as I did so a little black and white photograph fell out, revealing a young man whom I took to be John standing in a field which was on a bit of a slope, his hands together and his legs apart, reminding me of the way I would sometimes stand to have my picture taken, except that he was considerably smarter than me in his three-piece suit and his striped tie, and his hair, like his elderly brother's hair, neatly Brylcreemed, and indeed I reflected on how smart and tidy the other two had always been, and my grandfather still was. In this picture too, like so many pictures of Grandad when he was tall and slim, I was struck by how old John looked here, though he could not have been much more than twenty three, or perhaps not so much old as mature, wearing his suit in a way that I could only dream of, since a suit usually wore me rather than vice versa. It was the face, halfway between Arthur, the middle brother, and Olwen, the eldest sister, that persuaded me that this was John, and it took a while for me to get used to the new face, this new addition to the family, in my imagination, though he had actually been the first-born, so one might argue that the others' faces were variations on his rather than the other way around.

It was Summer, too, in the picture, or at least a fine day in Spring, because the bushes behind John were laden with foliage and the light was throwing sharply outlined shadows in that way in which all pictures of the past tend to give the impression that long ago the sun was always shining and the weather swelteringly hot. It was a small picture, not much bigger than a passport photograph, and that was why I hadn't noticed at first that the paper folded around it was a letter, and along with the picture were two cuttings from different newspapers, a local one from Llangedwyn and the other from a Manchester newspaper. The local paper recorded that John had moved to Manchester seven years before, that he had enlisted the previous year, that he had been drafted abroad in February, had been injured on the twenty-first of June and had died on the twenty-third. My guess that he had been a clerk at a Manchester booksellers was confirmed, and of course the paper was also eager to point out what a popular, respected, and academically successful young man he had been. I was struck, when I turned to the second cutting, by the irony that the piece from the Llangedwyn newspaper was in English, while the piece from the Manchester paper was in Welsh, its title particularly emotive, probably because the natural word order sounded, to my ear, as if it had been reversed, with the adjective placed before the noun,

Indeed, this piece was throughout the more tender and personal one, though it's possible that it seemed so to me because it was in Welsh, but the emphasis here was on the painful wait that his parents suffered between the time when they heard he had been wounded and the arrival of the telegram on Monday, 15 September, more than two months later, informing them that he had died, and as the short article stated, they had been very anxious about him, not knowing the extent of his wounds nor where he actually was. There was an additional emphasis here too on the fact that John had been a faithful and active member of Gore Street Methodist Church in Manchester, and through such details one got the feeling, despite the fact that they made a complete mess of the spelling of John's home back in Llangedwyn, that there was more empathy and fellow-feeling in that piece than the other.

But, after scrutinising the picture and the cuttings for so long, I had exhausted their meaning and significance, so it was now necessary to turn to the letter itself, and the next ones in the pile, namely two letters from John to Arthur, who had enlisted with the RAF but who was still, at that time, in Britain and had succeeded, to John's amazement and annoyance, in getting a fortnight's leave to return to Llangedwyn. One was dated Sunday, 6 June 1941, and the other Wednesday the nineteenth, and I felt a solid weight in my stomach when I realised that John had been mortally wounded three days after writing that letter. I felt, as I read those pencilled letters in their neat, small handwriting, that I was beginning to get to know the two brothers and their relationship to each other, indeed it was almost as if I were standing in the doorway, a mere silhouette against the bright light and so still that neither of the two had yet noticed my presence, eager to listen in on the whole conversation and yet knowing that something would come to interrupt the scene, that the two would hear the shuffle of my restless foot on the lino, or one of them would fail to answer, and fall silent.

Actually that had already happened in a way, because I had only John's side of the correspondence in my hands. Where was the partner of each letter, the other half without which no correspondence makes sense or is complete? In some breast pocket somewhere, and I felt uncomfortable when I realized that the one who had been alive was somehow the voiceless one in this one-way conversation, and that it was the one who had died whom I could hear, and that was precisely because he had died, and that his voice, his signature, had been cherished and kept alive because their owner had not been permitted to live. All of a sudden, I felt not like a playful eavesdropper but like a meddling trespasser and I felt the urge to slip away from the doorframe and to leave the two of them to their last, one-sided conversation. At the same time I felt a duty to stay in order to make a record of the conversation, to bring it to light. I find it impossible to bring myself to transcribe the letters, which are in English, but at least I ought to give an impression of the feelings, the longing, the emotion that I found within their folds.

In the first letter John talks of his sheer happiness when he received four letters on the same day, including one from Arthur, and then he is amazed that Arthur complains of the cold, while John himself, poor thing, was melting in the heat of the sun, and then he mentions his pleasure the day before when he saw a patch of green amid the endless sand. John enthuses about the food, but he is jealous that Arthur gets to meet his school-friends during his leave, and even goes to see a match with them, and that leads to a passage where he regrets that it seems like years since he saw a football match or even a film. But the letter is not without traces of enjoyment, as

John assures Arthur that it's possible to have a good time out there, and he is thankful that it's fairly quiet there at present, and he's been able to see a good deal through having to travel around so much. There's astuteness there too, since he suspects that Jerry, seeing that things were pretty quiet in the skies above England by now, probably had something 'up his sleeve', and the big brother's final piece of advice before signing off was for his little brother to 'keep his chin up'.

In the second letter, written during a brief stop as the troops are travelling through the desert, the men are 'out in the blue', their home is the truck and their ceiling the sky. In spite of that, what's striking about this letter is his interest in what's happening in Arthur's life, not in describing what's going on in his own, for John congratulates him on passing his exams, and hopes that they will soon be able to move on and even perhaps come out of the army, his tone that of the experienced older brother, advising and leading, and then he goes on to ask about those unimportant little details which were nevertheless full of a certain joie-de-vivre, such as whether Arthur had seen any good shows recently. At least John had seen a film, a 'talkie' even, called *The Broadway Melody of 1940*, again under the stars, and had enjoyed it inordinately since at least it had been a bit of a change. Then John starts to wind things up and to say good-bye, noting that he's trying to write as many letters as he can now because he knows that it will be a week or two before he gets a chance to send any more. Then, with a promise that he will write again soon, and adding as many x-shaped kisses as will fit into the line, John finally says farewell to his brother.

*

In 1904 the poet, author and, at the time, journalist, T. Gwynn Jones (TGJ) had been suffering for some time from severe depression, as well as physical illness, not helped, one imagines, by the pipe which he always had to hand, nor by the long hours of work he took on as he worked for a whole range of different papers, including the *Herald Cymreig*, the *Caernarvon and Denbigh Herald,* and that light but exceptionally interesting magazine, *Papur Pawb,* not to mention the fact that he would then, at night, disappear into his study for hours on end to toil over his literary works. It's not at all strange to find that he was jealous of John Morris-Jones, and envied him all the time he had to study and write in a leisurely fashion; by 1904, the Eisteddfod Chair he had won in 1902 for 'Ymadawiad Arthur' was just a pale memory, and the winter was proving long and cold as a bout of flu struck down the whole family in Dinorwig Street, and was threatening to turn into pneumonia in the case of T. Gwynn himself. He must already have been something of a hero for the people of Caernarfon, the so-called Cofis, because they collected money for a testimonial which enabled him to travel to Egypt to try to shake off the effects of the illness, and as I read about this I thought that I too would have been very thankful if someone were to make a collection for me to enable me to travel to a distant, exotic, hot country every time a cold threatened to take me down, but I managed to put aside my touch of jealousy and read on.

TGJ was quite a miserable creature, bordering on the melancholic and always convinced that people were against him, in addition to which he carried with him from an early age the strange burden of feeling that he was fated not to live long, that his life would be short, and perhaps that was why he forced himself to dedicate all his energy to every aspect of his literary and journalistic work, or perhaps, on the contrary, it was this constant fatigue that planted in him the eerie feeling that the life was being drained out of him much too quickly. Whatever the cause, the only thing that the extremely long journey to Egypt and his stay of some months' duration there achieved, though it did improve his health somewhat, was to deepen and intensify these negative emotions, and the death of his youngest brother, together with that of his friend and former teacher, Emrys ap Iwan, while he was thousands of miles away, did nothing but exacerbate his sense of complete powerlessness.

A more direct effect of these feelings upon him, in my opinion, was to kindle in him a deep and anguished longing for his wife and children, and also, for the landscapes and vistas of Wales, to such a profound extent that what he saw and encountered in Egypt from day to day tended to remind him, for a moment, of some place or occasion that he had once seen at home, which passed before his mind's eye like a shadow. The Arabian streets, as he called them, had reminded him of two lanes in Denbigh, Brombil Lane and Budur Lane, and a field of flowering bean plants, which he had ridden past on camel-back on an excursion to see the pyramids, had reminded him not only of a summer trip near Bodfari that he and his future wife, Meg, had once taken, but even the exact aroma and feel of the light breeze that had played with their hair on that day. At times, the view did not even have to be similar to give rise to this uncanny feeling in TGJ's mind, indeed it could be the precise opposite of what he was dreaming about, for he would remember, when he witnessed the beauty and splendor of Egypt's churches, how unadorned and bleak were the chapels of Wales, and this made a wave of extreme sadness wash over him.

The word 'dreaming' is really not so far from the truth for, when the coughing returned and he was finding it difficult to sleep in the extreme heat on the edge of the desert, he went through a spell of existing for some days in a state of semi-consciousness in which he could not be sure whether he was asleep or awake, and when he was convinced, on more than one occasion, that he was back on the very land and earth of Wales, smelling the salty air of the Menai Straits, walking along the sea front in Caernarfon with a loved one, although it had only been an open window, really, that had allowed a little breeze from the Nile to sneak into the pension and to penetrate his half-fainting state for a few seconds.

I remembered distinctly how I, too, as I travelled east through Europe and began to find each city more and more alike, and failing to sleep what with the jolting of the train and the frequent snores of this American and that Australian in this and that hostel, I began to be reminded by tiny details, such as the colour of a building or the bend in a river, of some place at home in the region of Caernarfon, and I found it more and more difficult to differentiate between my dreams, which grew more vivid every night, and the ceaseless walking and exploring I undertook during daylight hours. In Ljubljana, it had been the scrappy yellow-green grass on the banks of the river Ljubljanica that had reminded me of untidy clumps on the bike lane by the Menai, but then Cynon and I had caught a bus out to Koper to get a glimpse of the sea for the first time in weeks, and I couldn't stop myself turning my nose up at the pebbly beach which wasn't a patch on Dinas Dinlle, with the heights of Yr Eifl stretching out into the distance. For a while before we arrived in Prague, and for a short time afterwards, the nightly dreams appeared so clearly in my mind that I was living my life at night and had lapsed into a daytime state of anticipating dusk and the time to go to bed, so that I could once again fall into the deep slumber where my friends would be waiting for me, always the other side of the window of a bus which was about to leave, or in a doorway on the point of slipping out of the room, within reach and yet tantalizingly far off, or where my mother, my father, my brother and sister were waiting to take me to buy chips or, sometimes, where the sun was setting over the estuary and I was sitting on the wall outside the Anglesey, but I always woke up as I was about to take a sup of my pint. Occasionally the dreams would be cruel enough to create a mixture of the here and now and the distant there and then, as I walked across the Charles bridge over the Vltava arm in arm with this or that former lover or would-be lover, or I'd be slipping out of the pub, drunk, with her, our cheeks red from the cold beer and our hearts drumming in our chests, or she'd have texted or sent an email, and yet the following morning the phone would be silent and the inbox empty. More than once I was shocked in the course of these dreams to come face to face with someone who had not, to be honest, meant much to me before the journey, and yet was now the source of a bittersweet pleasure, and I tried to keep a hold of them as I slipped back into the waking world. At other times the border between these two worlds was abysmally clear, and I felt that my life was as if divided into two periods, namely the period before the journey, and the journey itself, and that it would be impossible for the two ever to touch or meet or cross over, and I couldn't imagine myself ever being back in the familiar surroundings of home, in the midst of these people, and then my homesickness would be excruciating.

That homesickness was worse, because it was more abstract, than the homesickness that came in the form of tears and was a kind of release, when I had got hold of a functioning phone and was able to hear the voices of my mother and father.

This homesickness was my only companion on the train from Moscow to Warsaw, when I was the only person in the carriage and the neighbouring one, apart from the ever-present *provodnitsa*, and I felt that we would never get through Belarus, while the soldiers had taken my passport away to examine it, and the whole train was shaking as we changed gauge. My mind insisted on running back along the tracks to a carriage, and a compartment, that was almost identical to this one, except that it was full of revelry, we four innocents pressed closely into our bunk beds among the disorderly Russians, the vodka being passed around much too quickly, and the train rushing towards Moscow, leaving the Urals far behind in the darkness, or further back than that even in the Gobi desert, lying awake with a silent blanket of sand spread out over everything – the tables, the beds, and the pillows, having squeezed its way in through the window frames during the night.

This was the homesickness that was intensified by the feeling of guilt which followed me from city to city because I knew full well how lucky I was to have this opportunity, with no ties and no responsibilities, being young and relatively well off, for the moment, and that I ought to be enjoying everything to the utmost until the guilt began to transmute itself into a feeling, almost, of duty, which succeeded only in strengthening the sense of déjà vu that was beginning to overwhelm me at every new station, on the banks of every river, over a black coffee in every piazza, every terrace. But I knew then that Cynon would be there to meet me in Warsaw in a couple of days, and I'd be able to speak Welsh to him properly for the first time for months, and we would be able to get drunk, and really it was only in those dreams and the sudden awakening from them that the homesickness came to disturb me for many weeks after that.

Because of that, I could dimly sympathize and understand a fraction of the emotion that had been poured into the ink of those words in John's letter as I read it, and I sought to comprehend how lonely under that sweltering sun he must have felt, with one brother in one corner of the world and the others at the very opposite corner; how much had he managed to conceal from Arthur in his succinct, matter-of-fact words, and how much had Arthur, like my own father, trying to read every little tremor in my voice through the crackle of the phone line when Mam passed the receiver over to him, managed to sense? That one sentence from the letter had stayed in my mind, the sentence that expressed John's desire to come back and see everyone, *if only for a few hours*, because I knew that I had written precisely the same desire more than once in my travel journal. I wasn't asking to return for a long time, to escape forever; indeed, I was convinced that, if I'd been able to spend one short hour with my family, and been able to do all those little ordinary things that I'd listed in the back of my book, watching a film or two, perhaps, among them, I believed that I could, then, have turned my back quite contentedly on it all and return to my journey where I had left off.

And yet, however much the moribund smell of the Nile had succeeded in convincing TGJ that he would never again fill his lungs with the seaweedy air of the Menai Straits, and however much my dreams had made me feel that I would never again be able to connect what I was, there, at that very moment, with a home that seemed faraway and unreal, in the end both of us had retraced our steps home. Unlike John, of course, and I wonder how full his dreams were of premonitions of that failure to return, and how full they were of some girl, or an image of Polly the mare, seeing him walking up the hill from the lane leading to the house, approaching him uncertainly, half remembering him but also realizing that this wasn't the same man as the boy who had left Canol Arren seven years previously. I'd been wondering, as I read his words, who or what exactly he'd been missing, and realizing that I actually had nothing approximating an answer to that question, I decided to embark on a journey, when the weather improved, to Canol Arren, to see with my own eyes whatever was left there of what once had been, and which was, in a way, still waiting for someone.

As things turned out, my chance to go there came sooner than expected, because a few months later I was in Llanuwchllyn, as part of a group of poets who were paid on occasion to perform in pubs and clubs, and I decided that I'd make my way across the Berwyn to Llangedwyn the next day in order to carry out my plan. However, I got to bed late and was therefore late getting up, and rather shamefacedly I felt some relief when I saw that it had snowed overnight and there was a layer of snow on the shores of Lake Bala, making the road over the Berwyn completely impassable. I had no choice, then, but to return to Caernarfon and hope that I would have another chance, when both my head and the road were much clearer, to visit my grandfather's old home, but as I returned home from Bala, I found myself again driving along the best part of the same route we used to take as a family to visit Grandma and Grandad in Llanfyllin and on which I had later served my apprenticeship as a driver, pushing the car to its limits, having just passed my test, to see just how fast I could navigate the bends of Cwm Prysor and then over to Cwm Celyn and Bala, before I started to see sense and slowed down a little on the perilous slopes of the Berwyn, and then I would come down slowly over many a cattle grid to the rolling hills of Maldwyn, and to the gentle undulations in the road through the valley.

Going in the other direction, then, leaving Llanfyllin

behind on the way to Caernarfon, I would usually need to go to the toilet shortly after going through Bala, and my fragile physical condition on this day, too, meant that I had to stop in the usual place, namely, beside Llyn Celyn. After I parked the car carefully in the parking bay where a thin layer of snow had begun to freeze, I stepped gingerly towards the toilet, and I saw the lake before me through the trees, surrounded by the hills and the white mountains, and before I relieved myself I went through the gate and down to the lake shore, in order to get a good look at the lake in all its glory. Its unaccustomed stillness, together with the fact that it reflected the overwhelming whiteness of the slopes around it and appeared strangely silvery, meant that it looked more than ever like a mirror, and I had to restrain myself from venturing onto the surface of the water since it looked so much as if it could be skated upon, and the tower at the other end of the lake looked like the dark silhouette of some rogue who had dared to step onto the lake but was now too shaky on his feet to attempt to make his way back to the safety of the shore.

I remembered once my brother and I, as we were returning from Llanfyllin, had stopped here and in the excitement of the realization that this was one of the first times we had been here without our parents, had undertaken that daring deed which it is the duty of every good Welshman to perform at some point in his life, namely to piss merrily into the lake, and we had felt quite proud of ourselves for doing so. I remembered also the pictures that my grandparents had of that fine day in the long hot summer of 1984, my grandad with his collar open and his knapsack hanging nonchalantly from one shoulder, his white cap at a jaunty angle, standing on the bridge in the village which was drowned beneath the waters but which had now, because of the drought, become visible as if yesterday were unveiling itself, and as if, should only a little more water evaporate, the post office and the chapel and the school could rebuild themselves, and the inhabitants would return home down the valley, like pressing the rewind button on a video machine. Then there was the picture of Grandma in a flowery dress, her hair with more grey than white in it and the frames of her glasses squarer than the ones she wore now; she too, it seemed, was subject to this process whereby everything was driven backwards, standing in one picture beside two skeletal tree trunks, half way back from being fossilized, or in another picture beside a mound of stones which looked like the ruins of some building or other but she was unable, now, to tell me exactly what it was. But she could remember that they had had a picnic, and she remembered too what that picnic had consisted of, namely individual salads in old margarine tubs, including lettuce and beetroot, some onion, corned beef, plenty of bread which, I imagine, would have been sliced very very thinly, according to grandma's usual practice, and spread with butter, making the sandwich that for me was unbeatable, because of the way it was cut and the way the butter was spread on it, though it came from an ordinary loaf and its filling was quite plain.

I could not imagine, and I dared not ask, whether Grandad had pissed into the lake that day, and today once more I did not dare to do the same thing because of my strange sense that the urine would simply splash off the surface of the mirror without sinking nor mixing with the water of the lake, but I did remember how appropriate the deed had felt that time with my brother, because it had given us a taste of the excitement, as we saw it, of those early protests and law-breaking, when the dam was only in its planning stage and the villagers were still trying to decide whether or not they were willing to let the bodies of their ancestors lie under the water. Because what came to one most strongly on the shores of the lake was not a feeling of respectable commemoration, or the sadness or tragedy of the drowning of Capel Celyn, but rather some tinge, once more, of jealousy, and that was the feeling that would rise up in me from time to time, as if from the depths of the lake itself, a feeling that I had been born in the wrong time, and that only the fact that I had not been born in the Depression of the twenties, or the language and human rights protests of the sixties, or even, perhaps, the periods of appalling suffering during the two world wars, was the only reason that I had not yet, according to my own estimation, succeeded in achieving anything in my life, or at least had not performed that one heroic act which would, in the course of time, come to define me and my generation.

Yes, I would, I persuaded myself as I stood on the shore of that lake, I would have been in the vanguard of the protest, with my placard held aloft and my voice raised hoarsely, if I had lived then. There was no point in my feeling guilty about doing nothing these days; hadn't the circumstances and the Weltgeist changed so much now, our lives being so comfortable that we could hardly comprehend adversity and poverty in the way that those other generations had done, and surely passionate protest about something nowadays would be mere overreaction and melodrama in the age of lobbying and public debate? As I made my way hesitantly back to the car, with my head still thumping and the journey home ahead of me still a long one, I said to myself that there was a good chance, had I been there at the time, that I too would have been among those who sat down on Trefechan bridge, or even one of those three who walked into the building site where the dam was being constructed and laid the bomb there, or even one of the three who burnt the bombing school to the ground.

You could almost describe these feelings that rose up in me from time to time like some sort of long-standing obsession with the various aspects of conflict and war, which had, since childhood, given rise to many meditations on what my own fate might possibly have been in a war of that nature. When I was a small boy, finding an old ARP warden's helmet and a gas mask in the garage at home had breathed new life into my games; putting on an old dark green nightgown and carrying a gun made of the inside of a roll of wrapping paper became a ritual from week to week, if not even more frequently. I would venture out into the field behind the house, where a patch of land that had been dug up in readiness to lay the foundations of a new building provided trenches perfect for my purposes. The events and reversals of the battle were always different, but one thing remained immutable – it was essential, somehow or other, whether as I crossed the ladder laid over the trench, or half way across the field, for me to get shot, or to be seriously wounded with a piece of shrapnel, or to trip and fall on my face onto a strand of barbed wire or into the bottom of a pit, and to die tragically. Even to my immature, childish mind, no narrative about trench warfare that I had come across had succeeded in convincing me that the odds in favour of my reaching the other end were healthy ones, and even if I had succeeded in doing that, the notion of reaching the Germans' trenches and then having to decide what to do then was something completely beyond my ken. The only option left was to die, to my mind, which made me consider further and ask myself how my childish imagination had been able to reconcile that immutable rule with the known fact that 'we' had won the war.

Only when I was older, and the games by this time taking place only in my imagination which would play like a film in my brain, did I start flirting with the idea that there was no reason why I shouldn't have been one of the lucky ones, who had succeeded by some miracle in avoiding the path of every shell and every bullet, and who had reached the trench at the other end of no man's land, stuck my bayonet through one or two German soldiers and held the trench, almost as if I was growing more naïve and self-confident in my own good fortune as my awareness of my own mortality increased. Later still, as I got older, I started to struggle with complex questions such as whether I could actually kill a man, whether I would be willing to fight, whether I would fight for an empire in whose cause I did not believe, and yet I knew that people at that time didn't think in this way, and certainly I would not have thought in this way either. I tried to put myself in that position when the call came, and I would be facing the inevitability, or at least the nearest thing to inevitability, of the fact that I was going to die, and I would ask myself whether that was how these boys had thought, or whether they believed innocently that they were about to go out and see the world and nothing more than that. I tried to consider whether that confidence in their own immortality and the unconquerable nature of their identities which suffuscd all the wild, drunken nights of my generation and of my group of friends in particular had also suffused these young children as they faced the destruction of their entire generation.

I questioned myself then, and perhaps this was the hardest question of them all, about what I would do if I knew that one member of the family would have to answer the call and leave. I remembered that story about Hedd Wyn refusing to let his younger brother go, although that brother wanted to enlist, and going himself instead to meet his death, acknowledging and acting upon his duty as the eldest brother, and John too, who was also an eldest brother in his family, leaving his two younger brothers and his sister behind in order to go, and to die, and he only twenty-four years old, and I tried to imagine it, knowing how many things I still wanted to achieve. I tried to imagine him walking, walking away, waving his cap, perhaps smiling.

This imaginary picture made me think of a photograph that my grandad had shown me, of three young boys in a hayfield, which was on a bit of a slant. On the left was a little figure about five or six years old, screwing up his face against the sun with his fingers knitted together, and he, my grandad's cousin, is standing somewhat apart from the two other figures. These two are on his right, one of them about eleven or twelve years old at a guess is sitting down, while the other no more than about two or three years old is standing up. The seated one is John, whose young face is recognizable from that other picture I saw of him when older and wearing a suit, and he has his arm placed protectively around the legs of my grandfather, an infant of two years. The eldest brother is smiling in a carefree manner and the youngest is frowning, and something in this indicated to me that he was trying to disentangle himself from this knot, perhaps because there was something too uncomfortable or too protective about it. That feeling I had when I watched Hedd Wyn in the film walking away and his brother left behind was crystallised in this picture.

Be that as it may, when I was a child I carried on playing though as I grew a little older I did wonder why I bothered and tortured myself with such morbid thoughts and notions, for there was certainly no need for me to imagine such things these days since the nature of the time was different, and indeed the nature of war itself had changed, and such evil men as Hitler no longer existed, and anyway people didn't allow them to proceed so far with their diabolical plans, and so in the fullness of time I stopped thinking such thoughts and I forgot about that boy who used to play trench war games in the field behind the house, facing his own ineluctable death time after time after time. By now, that kind of play and imagination would only come back to me on rare occasions, such as that afternoon on the shores of Capel Celyn, when it fell like a shadow across my mind, only to disappear once more.

PART 2

FEBRUARY 2012

By the end of the year, I had rather lost sight of the history of Uncle John, as I prioritized my research once again at the start of the new academic term. In the autumn, my increasing teaching duties also meant that any free time I had had to be given over to boring tasks such as lesson planning and marking, and in addition to that the period running up to Christmas proved to be full, as ever, of social events, so that, as the holidays approached, I found myself drinking more often and more heavily than usual, as well as gorging myself on winter treats, so that I started developing a beer belly. Just before Christmas, though, with the increasing hours of watching television that that entailed, my attention turned more and more to the media and the continual news reports on the conflict in Syria, which was quickly becoming the focus of the bloodiest fighting of the Arab Spring.

A number of experts were already predicting that the conflict would develop into a civil war, although there was no definite front that could be delineated on a map since the fighting flared up first here and then there, making it difficult to foresee where exactly the conflict would be fiercest next. It was becoming increasingly apparent though that the city of Homs and the surrounding area had suffered very badly, and increasingly stories reached us about the wretched state of the buildings, the transport system, and the severe shortage of food and water in the city. This war was by now having an extremely negative effect on civilians in the city and the country as a whole.

Lurking beside, or perhaps beneath, the feelings of horror and sympathy I felt about what was going on in Syria, were those old feelings with their mixture of guilt and envy. And yet these feelings did not lead to any noticeable outward changes in my behaviour, and my fits of taking an interest in the fate of Syria and feeling sorry for its people would come and go, particularly when work needed to be done and my own attention was far too easily distracted by various news websites. So, with this conflict as a constant if distant backdrop, I threw myself into my work once more in the new year, and it was only when I heard about the death of a journalist, Marie Colvin, the *Sunday Times* correspondent, as she was recording a broadcast about the siege of the city of Homs from a building that had been deliberately targeted, as was established later on, by the Syrian government forces because they knew that foreign journalists were working inside, that my attention was really forced to turn again toward Syria. Because of this death, the country's predicament, and especially the images of extreme suffering that the people of Homs were experiencing, suddenly appeared in all the news headlines, and heart-rending pictures by the French photographer, Rémi Ochlik, who was killed in the same attack, showing appalling scenes of widespread destruction, were plastered all over the front page of every newspaper and every news website.

It's strange to think, today, that it took the deaths of two western journalists, in this way, to make me realize, and to make many others like me, I'm sure, realize and understand how wretched the situation was in Syria by this time, and for some days afterwards I followed closely all the developments in the country, and in the wider region. As I followed it all I found that I was also feeling an element of relief that the fighting around Damascus was not yet too intense and that there was therefore a chance, even though I couldn't say for certain one way or the other, that the cemetery on the edge of that city was still in a reasonable state. So, it was being reminded in this way of my Uncle John's grave, together with the slow return of Spring to the land, that probably gave rise once more to that urge to travel in me, but it happened that money was exceptionally tight at the time, so that I had to admit that the whole project was impossible for the moment.

So, it was in a state such as this that I decided to

leave my work for a weekend and to travel home to Caernarfon to visit my parents, and to take advantage of the opportunity to talk to my grandparents about their experiences during the war, which would eventually shed light on some obscure areas and answer some questions I had after my perusal of the letters and booklet in the folder. Thus, it was on a dark, clear, cold Friday evening that I arrived in Bangor station, one of only a handful of travelers still on the train, which had been gradually emptied of its passengers over the previous stops, and there was my father waiting there to take me home. Coming home like this, and sitting down to supper with my parents and then watching television with them never failed to lift my spirits, and it was with a kind of energy that I hadn't felt for weeks that I made my way up to my old bedroom, which had remained almost exactly the same as it had been before I left to go to college for the first time, just a few weeks after the trip around Europe with Cynon, so much so that there were scraps of paper and coins from the various countries we'd visited still scattered about in small piles on my desk or on the carpet beneath my feet. My parents had often tried to get me to tidy these things away, but there was some indefinable comfort in returning time after time to this room where the bits and bobs, scenes, and even the merest hint of the smells of my last years as a teenager had insisted on remaining unchanged there, and I really had no desire, for the sake of clearing a small square of carpet, to put them away or throw them aside, since I wasn't yet ready to do so. I got up enthusiastically next morning as the low sunshine of early Spring flooded through the window in a way that it could not do amid the terraced houses of Cardiff; I gulped down a slice of toast and a cup of black coffee, and then walked, rather than take the car, down to my grandparents' house on the banks of the Menai. A thin layer of the last frost of the year had formed overnight and my feet crunched through the grass on the verge of North Road, and the Menai before me was still and blue, with just a small mound of sandbank rising above the surface of the water.

After I'd let myself into the house, calling hello in the usual way, I didn't hear the answering call I expected. The house was strangely quiet and still, and I immediately started to get worried. I called hello again, in a more questioning tone of voice, and again not getting any response I turned the handle of the kitchen door. There was no-one there and the oven was cold, but the back door was ajar, and so I ventured through it and through the small utility room into the back garden, and still found no-one, but as I turned the corner I saw my grandmother squatting down digging in the earth. 'Already at it, Grandma?' I said, and without being at all alarmed or even changing the tempo of her slow digging with the trowel, she replied that there was no time like the present, that it was really too fine a day to be stuck in the house, and that it was high time, to be honest, to get the garden into shape ready for the summer. 'Where have you hidden Grandad, then?' I said, and she answered, 'Oh, the foreman has already had quite enough. He's fiddling with that old camera in the study, I can't imagine why he thinks it's still going to work.'

On hearing this I pricked up my ears and left her for the time being and went to look for Grandad, finding, as I stepped back into the house and into the living room, that he was there, with earphones on, and since he was fairly hard of hearing at the best of times, it was no wonder that he hadn't heard my usual greeting five minutes earlier. He turned, though, when he heard the door opening, greeted me with a smile, and urged me to go and take a look at what he was doing. I was astonished to find that he had succeeded in connecting an old Super 8 camera to a projector with a small screen that he had also found among the bits and pieces in the study, and had managed to get it to work.

It had been quite an undertaking, some five years before, when I helped my grandparents move house to Caernarfon in order to be closer to us, because of the way that fifty years' worth and more of artefacts, each one in its own way a witness to family and conjugal life, had accumulated in their house, and they were all surprisingly difficult to get rid of, despite the fact that they acknowledged that they were completely unremarkable bits and pieces. Most of these things had been gathered in the two poles of the house, as it were, in the attic and the cellar, and in the latter particularly, where all of Grandad's tools and utensils were piled up higgledy-piggledy on the workbench and on the cold, black floor around it, all on top of each other, shovels and screwdrivers, saws and tins of paint and oil and who-knows-what besides, and then there were Grandma's jam jars in a never-ending row on the shelves. Had Grandma not had her way, the majority of these things would have found their way to Caernarfon with Grandad; and if mam, in her turn, had not had *her* way, a large number of pointless objects would have followed Grandma too to the Cofis' town.

As things turned out, they had been forced to select and discard, but even when some little things were destined for the bin, such as that wooden, wood-worm-eaten butter press that used to be an ornament on the stairs, my sister and I managed on the sly to salvage it and to throw it in the back of the car, so between us all we ensured that we had a lot of work fetching and carrying. Perhaps the most important consideration was that by the time my grandparents had settled into their new house on the banks of the Menai, it contained enough of the old things all around them that we were persuaded that the two of them hadn't really moved at all, but had been living in this new house forever. Even that sweet, stuffy smell, and the hint of dust underneath it, had come with the move, and both the garage and the study, and even the little porch behind the front door, despite all the effort and the good intentions, were now once more like barns full of the harvest of their lives, and primarily the desert-like expanses of Grandad's stuff.

It was there, in the study, then, that Grandad had found this old camera when some desire to potter came over him and he had discovered it and set it up. And now here we were, the two of us, watching old film reels in the living room and I don't really know why Grandad had been wearing those earphones when I came in because the only thing that you could hear was the purring of the film revolving rapidly, frame by frame, and the pictures were extraordinarily similar to that video I had made of the orchestra in Florence, except that these were no digital effects. And yet there was a likeness in the fragmented nature of the film, and the way it jumped from clip to clip with no warning and no commentary, and I don't know whether Grandad had been listening in case there was some trace of his own voice speaking over the pictures, explaining what was going on, or whether perhaps he was listening out for the voices of his own children when they were five and eight years old. For that was the first scene, a scene showing Grandma, whom I recognized immediately despite the fact that her hair was dark and her face much rounder, and also my uncle, wearing short trousers, and my mother, though I didn't recognize her for some moments, wearing a flowery dress and with one of her front teeth missing, her plaits framing her face, and the three of them sitting together on a hillside. Maldwyn was glittering in different tints of green in the summer sunshine, and everything was bathed in that golden light, the one that seems to shine in every old picture. The three of them were smiling rather shyly at this new camera, which was a marvel to them, and to which they didn't quite know how to react, as if they couldn't wait for Grandad to switch the blooming thing off so that they could get on with behaving naturally, and you could almost see the relief on their faces as the camera panned across towards Uncle Arthur, tall and well turned out as ever, like Grandad, like the three of them, wearing a suit and tie even on a sweltering hot day like this one, and the Brylcreem on his hair gleaming in the sun.

Then the scene jumped, without warning or explanation, to a group of people standing outside a building, and it took me a few seconds to realize that it was in front of Tabernacle, my grandparents' chapel in Llanfyllin, that this crowd of about twenty or thirty people were standing, a crowd ranging from little boys in shorts and girls with ribbons in their hair to respectable old ladies in flower-sprigged dresses and grandiose hats. Again that light held sway, making me think that it was some kind of effect it was possible to add to the film later, in order to make every day look like a long, golden summer's day, but no, in the corner of the screen you could sometimes catch a glimpse of the brook flowing past the chapel which seemed full of sparks as the sun shone brightly upon it, and the women smiled as if there were no tomorrow and as if pain did not exist.

But when I saw that colour again later, with its total authenticity that almost seemed to betray its own kind of deception, rather than making everything more lifelike it seemed to make it more unreal, like those pictures I had seen from time to time of First World War soldiers, or peasants in the depths of Siberia at the end of the nineteenth century, in full colour. These scenes were supposed to be in black and white, because that's how we were accustomed to and expected to see them, and the moment I realized that the very same colour I could see in a piece of my own clothing had also existed on the hem of a dress worn by a hard-faced peasant woman standing on her doorstep in the region of Irkutsk in 1909, the past would come and disturb my own present in a way which was much too real.

It was the same with that row of girls in front of the chapel in Llanfyllin, because somehow or other it took the fact that they were now getting on in years, and that middle-aged Grandma standing beside them looked exceptionally young, to make me realize how long ago this scene was and that the oldest among this crowd were not contemporaries of my grandparents, and indeed that one half of the happy married couple now emerging from the murk of the doorway, smiling and screwing up their eyes against the sun, was already dead. I sat there listening to Grandad, and to Grandma, who had just come in from her gardening with some smudges of earth still on her face where she had wiped it with her hand, and had sat down wearily in her armchair, the two of them egging each other on and naming everyone who smiled at them in the film, noting whether they were still alive or not, and the vast majority of them had passed on long ago. I was struck then by the thought that I had no comprehension of this, the experience of seeing all the people I had once known, but who had now disappeared, who no longer existed except on a reel of shaky Super 8 film or in vague memories, and I couldn't decide whether this would give rise to a feeling of good fortune that one had survived, or perhaps a feeling of loneliness, and I realized then that the simple act of sitting there watching it all and naming, and stating that this man or that woman had died, was one of the loneliest things a person could do.

When the film was over, the last frame of Grandma

smiling by the seaside in Jersey jumping suddenly into darkness, I realized that I hadn't seen my grandfather in any of the pictures except for a brief glimpse of him, holding a thin fag in his hand, for a second or two between two longer clips, because he was almost always behind the camera. I don't know if it was the fact that he was strangely absent from every picture, though everyone's gaze was almost invariably directed at him and they were looking at him with that strange, deeply embarrassed smile on their faces, or the fact that, when I questioned the two of them, they couldn't remember who was behind the camera for that brief second when he himself was the star, nor what the occasion was, nor could they make out enough of the background to be able to say where it had been even, that so unsettled me. But it was time to put away the projector and the Super 8 because it was dinner time, and I got to my feet to help put the camera and the rest of the equipment back in the empty space that had been left in the study, among the other dusty boxes.

That study was a remarkably interesting place, having as it were taken on the character of the old attic and cellar simultaneously, and therefore full of an even more extraordinary mixture of things. Near the light switch on the way out of the room, under some old blue ice-cream tubs full of elastic bands and paper clips and old pocket diaries and magnifying glasses, was a pile of scrapbooks and hardback photograph albums, which I decided to pick up carefully and put to one side with the intention of looking through them in more detail after dinner. But at the bottom of the pile, almost as if it had been placed there to be compressed, like a metamorphic rock, was another book, a paperback this time, and for some reason I was drawn to it and I put it on the table in order to look through it.

When I opened it, I saw that the paper cover was fragile and liable to tear in my hands, and so I took greater care as I turned the dry, brittle pages, almost as if I were handling a manuscript in a library, and I found that every page in the little book contained a flower or plant, which had been dried and pressed, and had been attached there with sticky tape which had itself by now dried in yellows and browns. There were dozens and dozens of various plants, many of them by this stage having faded or lost their colour completely so that it would have been impossible to differentiate much among them, except that they were named, and these names had been written in carefully in Grandma's tidy handwriting in the bottom corner of every leaf: foxglove, bluebell, tiny fragile snowdrops, honeysuckle and forget-me-not, meadowsweet, peony and saxifrage, shepherd's purse, lavender and heather, primrose and daisy, ox-eye daisies and old man's beard, clover and broom. They were all there, but my fingers paused on those last two names, which reminded me of something that I couldn't quite recall, but as I turned the page I saw a little sprig of rosemary placed across the card under a dried-up layer of sticky tape, and I suddenly remembered the occasion weeks earlier when I'd read that description of the cemetery in Syria in the register of graves included in the folder, and the detailed entire paragraph that was given:

In the older part of the cemetery an avenue of Judas trees leads from each of the two shelters to a seat at the other end, low rosemary hedges define the grave plots and around it are pepper trees and cypresses. In the new portion beds of oleanders grow to the left of the entrance and there are various groups of flowering shrubs which include hibiscus in variety, arbutus, myrtle, Etna broom and caryopteris.

Quite remarkable and unexpected to my mind, was the fact that the different plants that grew there were described in this way.

After dinner Grandma and I went back into the garden while Grandad went to snooze in front of the television; I squatted down to do the work of digging and weeding while Grandma looked on, sometimes encouraging me but more often criticizing, since I was holding the trowel wrongly or doing the job too hurriedly, without taking time to take out every tiny leaf of weed and every piece of gravel. Partly because that litany of names, as well as the book of pressed flowers, was still running through my mind, and partly because I wanted to distract Grandma's eagle eye from my digging, I ventured to ask her about the book and some of the flowers within it. She smiled in reply, and I asked again what the story of the little book was, but she was more interested in where I had managed to find it, since she herself had not laid eyes on it for some years, and certainly not since they moved house, because it was a very old booklet, 'older than you', said Grandma, 'and almost as old as your mother, because it was when she was very young that she and I collected all the flowers you saw in the book, and then we dried and pressed them, and put them away.'

Eventually the two of us went into the kitchen for a cup of tea. I went to look for Grandad but the television was blaring and he was snoring, so on my way back I went to the study to fetch the book, and Grandma and I looked at it together over our tea and coffee, she pausing at this flower and that, remembering exactly where she had picked it, or saying 'yes, I was on my way back from the school, and your mother was delighted when I brought this home for her', or again that piece of yellow broom that Mam and she, and her own mother, had picked on the steep slopes above Troed yr Ewig one morning. 'What about this rosemary, Grandma?' I asked, beginning to cross-examine her about some of the plants mentioned in the description of the cemetery, and she said 'oh yes', she hesitated, and then 'wait a minute, I was with your grandad when I found this one, when we were on holiday in Rhodes once, and I took it without telling anyone', she explained, 'and I put it in the bottom of my suitcase and brought it back here to Wales. That's why this is here in the back, you see', she said, 'because it was added later on', and indeed when I looked more closely I could see that this sprig looked a little fresher, and we both leant a little closer to the leaf, almost as if we could smell it once more. 'They say', said Grandma, 'that rosemary can improve your memory', and I thought that there could be a shred of truth in that, considering how well my grandmother could remember where she had found each of these little flowers, and indeed I suddenly remembered then some of the other names from the list of plants in the cemetery.

I had already read about the cypresses, and the Judas tree with its dark pink blossom, and had found out the Welsh names for *arbutus* which were the equivalent of strawberry tree. But the *hibiscus* continued to puzzle me, even after consulting various books that we had in the house, because it seemed that there was a large number of different species to be had under this umbrella term, and one of them was the *Hibiscus syriacus*. That name struck me immediately, of course, and I was convinced that that was the specific *hibiscus* that grew in the cemetery in Damascus. When I read more about it later, I learnt that some believed, though it was by no means an accepted fact, that this was the rose of Sharon mentioned in the Bible, but that no-one today could say with any certainty which plant was really meant by that name. When I discovered that, and saw the name in the list so close to the myrtle, the words of that hymn:

See him standing 'mid the myrtles
worthy object of my love.
…

The Rose of Sharon is his name,
White and blushing, fair of face

Immediately came back to me. I wasn't entirely sure
about the myrtles either, and I noticed that I hadn't
seen either of these plants in my grandmother's book.
So I ventured to ask 'what about myrtles, Grandma?',
and she said, less in answer to my question than as
a kind of instinctive reflex or reaction, 'See him
standing 'mid the myrtles', almost like some kind of
meditative note to self, exactly as I had done when I
read the word 'myrtle' too. She wasn't sure, however,
about the plant and its details, so she had to reach
for her little book of flower names, with its beautiful illustrations which divided them into categories,
oddly, according to their colour, tint, and shading,
and Grandma would swear that there was such a
thing as a yellow marsh mallow, despite the fact that
the illustration in the book was pink. 'To tell you the
truth, Grandma', I said 'I wanted to ask you about
the rose of Sharon too, as it happens,' and she rose
to her feet at once and gestured through the window
saying 'there's one of those growing in the corner
over there, do you see?', but she could not confirm
that this was the *hibiscus* that I had seen in the cemetery book.

Grandad walked into the kitchen from the front
room and sat down slowly in his chair, Grandma
turned from the window towards him, suddenly saying 'Myrtles, Da?' to which he mumbled 'Mm?' in

return, being clueless, since he had only just woken up, of what she was talking about, but then after he steadied himself a bit and processed the word in his mind, he said 'See him standing 'mid the myrtles'. It was then that I was struck by the immense importance and the central role that hymns had had in my relationship with my grandparents, and the connection they had created between us across three generations, which went deeper than the fact that they used to like, when I called in, to drag me to the piano to stumble my way through some hymn tune or other, though I was not at all proficient, and they would sail on singing to the end of the verse despite the fact that I was still struggling about the middle of the second line. This realization had already started to dawn on me when I was looking through some leaflets which were with the bundle of letters in the folder and found a number of funeral cards for different members of Grandad's family. Once a few years ago I had asked the two of them what their favourite hymn was, and they had replied, in unison, that 'One blessing give to me' to the tune of 'Sirioldeb' ('Serenity') by Joseph Parry was their favourite, and I had taken it for granted that it was the loveliness of the words and the tune themselves, added to the fact that Grandma had once won first prize for a solo at Powys Eisteddfod when she sang that hymn, that accounted for the evident delight that both of them took in it, affording it little importance to such an extent indeed that I would pull Grandma's leg by repeating the words of the first line of the hymn to a completely different tune, and would take pleasure in seeing her and Grandad telling me off then and swearing that the words didn't fit that tune at all.

Not until the hymn was sung in Uncle Arthur's funeral did I begin to take it seriously and it began to acquire a deeper significance in my own mind. It gave me a bit of fright when I looked through those funeral cards again later, and realized that this particular hymn was sung in the vast majority of the funerals in Grandad's family, ranging from Nesta, the little girl who died of diphtheria at the age of eight, to the father, John Morris, and the mother, Elizabeth Jane, who was the last of them to die. I saw then the way in which hymns gained layers of meaning until the original words sometimes became almost irrelevant, or at least less relevant unless all the occasions on which the hymn had been sung and the memories attached to those occasions were taken together, and the notes would be heard echoing from funeral to baptism to wedding to singing festival, and from chapel to chapel to the brink of the grave. And yet somehow, the words of the poet Eifion Wyn still had significance, and that desire to 'have grace to love the Lord forever' and, in times of sadness, 'to rest upon his breast', somehow sounded more earnest and more poignant, more full of pathos, to think of all the suffering that had been loaded upon them by decades-worth of funerals.

Another hymn which had had quite an effect

on me, which I hadn't noticed until comparatively recently, was George Rees's hymn to the tune 'Guidance'. A few months after Grandad gave me the folder, but before I read its contents, I was in chapel one dark, rainy Sunday night when the congregation rose to sing this hymn, and I felt, as I asked God to give me the great vision 'to turn me from my foolish wandering', some inexplicable and overwhelming need to weep, until by the last verse

You are the way, and more than the way for me,
you are my strength:

I was literally struggling to hold the tears back. I gave silent thanks for the fact that this was the last hymn, and I made my escape quickly that evening into the safe darkness of the night without exchanging a word with anyone, and I was perplexed for some days afterwards about this sudden and irrational wave of emotion which had swept over me. I was quite surprised, then, when I came upon a little card which bore the inscription

MEMORIAL SERVICE
In Loving Memory of John Owen Jones who
passed away
in the Middle East while serving his Country,

to find that it was this very hymn, with its vivid description of the One who knew nothing of losing heart, but who reached the end of his costly adventure through great suffering, that was sung at the end of that service too, and I wondered then, though the thing was highly unlikely from a rational point of view, whether there was a part of me or some element of my genetic inheritance which *knew* that somehow, and that was responsible for the sudden wave of emotion I experienced when I took notice of this hymn for the first time, or was it simply attributable to the chilling combination of a sad tune and the raw but emotional words? Even today there's something in me that is convinced that that hymn, just like the hymn sung to the tune 'Serenity' except in a very different way, had also given rise to a plethora of meanings in me from a distance of fifty years or more, and that I had heard some weak echo of the deep groan and the fractured cry calling me home, prodigal son that I am.

When my grandparents said those words, 'See him standing 'mid the myrtles', that day, I was reminded of the occasion, a few months before they moved from Llanfyllin, when they were still relatively agile, and I had offered to take them for a spin around the neighbourhood in the car, there having recently been some stormy weather so that the river and the waterfall that we visited thundered past us, and I realized gradually that it was them taking me for a trip, though I was in the driver's seat, as they named every hill and lane, and we went past the chapel at the top of the hill. They used to go and sing there at a singing festival once a year, one of them approaching it from one direction and the other from the opposite direction, at a time when they still did not know each other except from afar, as familiar faces; Grandma also pointed out the steep hill she used to have to climb every day with her bike to school, and when the car zoomed past an old village hall Grandad announced proudly that it had been he, with a small group of four others, who had built that hall with their own hands. The entire neighbourhood, though they had not traversed and crossed it like this for years, was at the tips of their fingers, the map of it clear in their heads and the names of people and places woven together as the car climbed and descended the hills of Maldwyn, and they enjoyed debating with each other whether so-and-so was now dead or who was living these days in that farm or other.

Though I had no inkling of this at the time, I could see when I looked at the map later that we had travelled quite a distance in two different directions from Llanfyllin that day, firstly, not far from that river and waterfall, to visit the Ann Griffiths Memorial Chapel in Dolanog, where a bust of the hymn-writer from Dolwar Fach made quite an impression on me, because of the whiteness of the plaster it was made of, which made it seem almost like a ghost, and because it was set at the base of one of the rafters, as if her spirit were in some quite literal way sustaining the place, preventing it from falling down and keeping it upright. It was a rather strange building from the out-side, with its dark stone and its high pointed gables, as if it couldn't quite make up its mind whether it was a chapel or a church, and with its round porch protruding from the front of the building almost like the turret of a warship.

Grandad provided me with something of the history of the construction of the place, while Grandma sang a snatch of a hymn now and again, and the three of us signed our names in the visitor book, before shutting the door quietly after us and walking back to the car. Inspired or spurred on, perhaps, by our visit to the chapel, my grandparents then insisted on giving me directions on how to get to Dolwar Fach itself, Ann Griffiths's home, and eventually the poor car, after negotiating a somewhat uneven and pot-holed lane, landed up in front of a farmyard which it wasn't possible to get beyond nor get into, since the way was barred by a large wooden gate that was firmly closed. I undid my seat belt, ready to go and knock on the door, but the two of them, who for some reason had chosen to sit together in the back seat rather than have one sitting beside me, told me not to, claiming that the family in the farm surely wouldn't want strangers like us coming to knock on their door all the time, and saying that the fact that the gate to the farmyard was closed was in itself a sign that the present owners of the farm didn't want anybody disturbing them.

And so we went back to the main road, and I continued to receive a kind of never-ending running commentary from the two in the back as well as directions on how to get to Sycharth, where Owain Glyndŵr once had his court. We approached Llangedwyn from the west, before passing through the village and turning towards Llansilin. The two of them knew exactly where to go, and before long we had parked the car in the vicinity of a farm, but when we reached the gate on the footpath that led up the mound, Grandad found that it was locked, and so the three of us retraced our steps to the farm, following the instructions on the gate, in order to get permission from the farmer. But we failed to find anyone around there so the three of us had to content ourselves with admiring Sycharth and the half-circle of trees that grew around it from a respectable distance, from the point of view of the attacker rather than the defender, the patron, the guardian. From that position, and with the frustrating obstacle of the locked gate in front of us, and indeed, perhaps with the frustration of being there with them, since I could have jumped over the gate to climb to the summit quite easily, without being seen, I could also empathise, however, with those in this position feeling just how terrifying and impregnable these old forts could appear, as well as appreciating how welcoming the fort would have felt to a young whippersnapper of a bard with no patron or an exhausted traveler as he rounded the bend on his way down from the mountain pass and saw the might of the structure in the valley before him. 'Don't worry', Grandma said to me as we got back into the car, 'you'll be able to come back here by yourself one day'.

After we'd strapped ourselves in once more, Grandma and I were ready to head back to Llanfyllin, but as I turned the key in the ignition, Grandad said quietly 'wait a minute', and said that there was one more place he wanted to visit. After going just a stone's throw towards Llanfyllin, then, I turned the car around again and went along a narrow lane that led up the hill, this time, following it for some time higher and higher, before the hedge gradually fell away allowing us to see before us on the slope a field of substantial acreage, with a small house at its far end, and though neither of the two had said anything, I knew then that we had come back to Canol Arren. In my imagination, the house had been black and white, of course, but this house had some kind of dull green pebbledash on its façade, while the double windowframes and the PVC doors were all white, so that it appeared like a home which couldn't be more than thirty or forty years old. I don't know for sure why the fact that the house had been renovated in this way caused me such sorrow, for I should have been glad, I suppose, that it was still some-body's home and a home of which the owners clearly took care. This unexpected transformation of a place that I had never known in its original state unsettled me to such an extent that I was almost convinced that I would have preferred to see it in ruins or with just a few traces left of its existence, and in considering the matter further that uneasy feeling was all the more irrational since at that time I had no clear idea of the history of the place nor a consciousness of its importance.

My state of distress was exacerbated by the fact that my grandparents did not get beyond the gate that separated the drive from the road, a gate without which it would have been impossible to tell where one ended and the other began, but that had been the case with so many of the other places we had visited that day, either because they weren't able or weren't willing. There's a picture of us as small children in one of the albums at home, or perhaps, mulling it over, it's a picture of the family of my uncle (my mother's brother) when they were children, standing in front of this house, and I had never made the connection with Canol Arren when I had looked at it before that day, but that in itself was a consolation, to think that my grandparents had, once, ventured further than the gate and had even, perhaps, dared to knock on the door, had explained that this was my grandad's childhood home, and had asked to be allowed to look around. On that day, however, the two of them refused point blank, though I myself volunteered to go and knock and explain, while Grandad insisted from the back 'no, there's nobody at home, I'll bet'. Of course there was nobody at home. For Grandad, there had been nobody at home for half a century or more.

I don't know if I imagined it then, a sudden whiff of rosemary that awoke my memory and brought me back to the present, but I was back again in my grandparents' kitchen in Caernarfon, and Grandma was saying that I could take that book home with me, as well as the pocket book containing all the little illustrations of different flowers. When I sat down at my desk at home, and read again that description of the flowers in the cemetery, and searched through the book and online for more information about the flowers, I couldn't stop thinking about that putative rose of Sharon, that *hibiscus syriacus*.

I came across pictures of it, and among all the varieties that existed, I was particularly struck by the Red Heart, a striking flower because its petals were completely white, except for a stab of dark, velvety red in the middle, like the red heart of its name, or as if a drop of blood had accidentally fallen on it, even, and that impression was strengthened by the fact that thin lines of red radiated out from the centre. That immediately made me think of that description in the medieval romance, *Peredur Son of Efrog*, which is about Peredur going out of the hermit's cell and finding that there had been a fall of snow during the night. Peredur finds a dead bird, and he stands there, mesmerized somehow by what he sees, and he compares the blackness of the crow, which has been feasting on the dead bird's flesh, the whiteness of the snow and the redness of the blood to the woman he loved the most, for her hair was as black as jet, her skin as white as snow, and her cheeks as red as the blood on the snow.

Just as Peredur meditated upon those things, so did I upon the *hibiscus syriacus*, and it occurred to me how ironically apt it would be if the 'Red Heart' turned out to be the one that grew in Damascus, not only because of the name but because it would seem almost as if the lads had been wounded only a moment ago, their blood had not yet dried on the petals of the flowers, and there might still be time to save them. Then I thought how inappropriate the myrtles would be in comparison, because from what I read about the *myrtus,* it had been used for many centuries as a symbol of love and of immortality, two concepts called into question by the very existence of that cemetery, unless the myrtle offered some kind of reassurance or hope to the mourners that a kind of love and immortality were to be found in the next life, since they had not been found in this one. As I mulled this over, I asked myself why exactly people had, for thousands of years, used flowers as emblems of commemoration. Because they signified fertility, giving assurance of the coming of every season in its turn, of the ending of that season, and its return once again, perhaps. Or simply, one might admit, to conceal the stench and rottenness of death with a veneer of colour and perfume.

Whatever the reason, I was transported back to that evening near Ieper when Cynon and I had returned, after a day spent among the graves, to the bed and breakfast place in Brandhoek, a village some four or five miles out of the town past Vlammertinge. It was kept by an amiable and kind middle-aged couple, Liz and Jon, not to mention Sambo their black

Labrador, who had left their comfortable lives in England to come and run the Cherry Blossom B&B. The two of them worked hard, Jon having to work behind the bar in a pub in town as well as helping Liz at home, just in order to make ends meet, but there was a sense of quiet contentment about them, and Cynon and I felt the same quiet happiness coursing through our bodies, too, as we ate our steaks and drank our bittersweet Trappist beer. I wonder what had prompted them to call the place Cherry Blossom? It didn't occur to me to ask them at the time. Later Jon, Cynon and I sat out in the back garden with Sambo, and though it was getting dark it was warm enough for us to sit there in our T-shirts, before even Cynon was forced to give in and reach for a jumper, and as the three of us talked we looked out beyond the garden over the flat fields of Flanders, where, two or three fields in the distance, we glimpsed blurred flashes of red as the poppies in the fields undulated in the light evening breeze.

We could almost hear the seeds rattling in their capsules, and we could certainly hear the dogs of the neighbourhood barking in the silence that descended suddenly upon us, but eventually Jon and Sambo retired to bed, leaving Cynon and myself to watch the moon set behind a nearby row of cypress trees. After a spell of silence, which remained as if the two of us were acknowledging the meaning of the silent scene before us, as it disappeared into the total blackness of night, we gradually slipped back into conversation, and I don't know whether it was the sound of the breeze in the poppies that had brought a note of regret or nostalgia or recollection to our conversation, or some kind of momentary longing for the moment itself which was already slipping through our fingers, but there was a tacit recognition on both our parts, as we talked of our childhood, that we were children no longer, and that we would both be going our separate ways when the new academic year started. We went through everything, with almost scientific thorough-ness, talking about home, about school, about what was to come, about love, and beneath everything was the consciousness of memory, the knowledge that on the one hand we were a thousand times more fortu-nate than those who had fallen in these very fields and who were, possibly, still lying beneath our feet, but on the other hand and simultaneously we were aware that there was something in ourselves which had passed away, or was on the brink of passing, and which would not be with us when we arrived home.

*

Some weeks after that visit to my grandparents, I decided to go by train to London for a few days. I wasn't entirely sure why I was so keen to go on a whim like this, beyond a half-baked plan to find some information about the movements of John's regiment in the National Archives in Kew, along with the sense that a random trip to London, one of my favourite cities in the world, was a pretty good idea in itself and that it offered a welcome change from everyday work at my desk. After I'd changed trains in Crewe and eaten the sandwich I'd bought on the platform, England was rolling past us faster and faster and the carriage was swaying at an angle on the curves. The weather, like the landscape, was changeable, so that I thought one minute that the sun would be shining all day from an azure blue sky, the next minute we were hurtling towards a threatening dark raincloud. The land was already drenched with the rain of the previous months, and every river I saw was threatening to break its banks.

Then we were passing through the suburbs, past the backs of supermarkets, industrial estates, and patches of waste ground where the concrete was being overgrown by weeds reclaiming their former place, and somewhere in the no-man's-land between these grey suburbs and the lush greenness around them were the factories, where I once saw six gigantic cooling towers ranged in two rows of three, belching out their smoke in remarkably neat columns, before those columns became elongated and dispersed, disappearing into the air, and I spent quite some time, while the towers were still within sight, puzzling over where exactly the smoke became cloud, and vice versa, and musing on how alike these two entities were to each other, to such an extent that it really wasn't possible to differentiate between them with the naked eye. Normally, seeing such towers, or looking at similar industrial scenes of factories and unhealthy growths on the green of the landscape would fill me with an indefinable but intense sense of horror and unease, but somehow these towers didn't arouse the same fear in me this time, in spite of the grey clouds which continued to accumulate behind them, and before long the buildings became taller, and the houses narrower, the bricks lighter and therefore showing more clearly the grime of decades' worth of trains going past them, the architecture became older, and the train was slowing and creeping into Euston station.

This was the first intercity railway station to be built in London, though it was now less busy than five of the other big stations which are situated, like orbiting satellites, around the centre of the city. It was built in 1837, and the magnificent stone structure known as the 'Euston Arch' was added soon after, while the Great Hall which was, apparently, an impressive space, was divided into different levels, and with its rectangular windows (not too ornate), its Ionic columns, its heavy wooden doors, its carved ceiling, and its central staircase which divided into two on the right and the left before coming together again at the bottom, it tended inevitably to remind one of the inside of a Nonconformist chapel. I wondered if my uncle John, too, had been struck by that resemblance, assuming that he had passed through this station with his regiment on their way to France, before they were driven back by the German forces, something which was perfectly possible, though I didn't know for sure. Or did he notice in particular, after he had travelled here from Manchester where he lived, the sculpture which represented that distant city, one of a series of eight set around the interior walls of the station portraying the various cities – Liverpool, Manchester, Birmingham, and their like – which were sending their travellers en masse to this station at the very centre of the empire? Would he have taken his first steps out into the city through the doric columns of this arch?

It was hard for me to imagine this scene, how-ever, and it was not the scene that I encountered, for the old magnificent station had been pulled down unceremoniously and against stiff opposition at the beginning of the sixties, in order to make way for the rectangular black and grey concrete box that occupies the site now, being one of the newest and most mod-ern among all the great stations today, and serving as an example of that brutalist concrete architecture of the sixties which nowadays is almost universally despised. Since I got to know the magnificence and excitement of St Pancras, and the wide-open bustle of Paddington, where there's no division between the main hall and the platforms except the ticket gates erected fairly recently, quite different from Euston where the main hall is completely closed off from the platforms under its black ceiling, I too could under-stand and agree with those opponents and critics of what had been done here.

And yet there was a special magic to this place for me because it was here that we used to arrive as a family years ago, shortly before Christmas usually, to spend a weekend, and I remembered my parents struggling to get us all off the train and bundled into a taxi, or that time in the mid-nineties, when I was a child of eight with an over-active imagination, frightened almost to death just thinking of going to London at a time when some mysterious people called the Ayareh posed a constant threat of terrorist explosions; we had had to wait in the train outside the station because of a 'bomb scare', or that other time when there had been 'an incident involving a person on the tracks' and my parents had to try to explain to us three, without going into too much detail, why we were still waiting around and taking it in turns to sit down amid our bags and cases in the middle of the great hall, on the shiny, marble-like floor patterned in black and grey, as we gazed, open-mouthed at the vast concrete ceiling, tracing its crisp, clean lines.

A fit of sadness descended on me as I arrived this time, paced through that hall, and turned for a moment to glance over my shoulder and found that the arrival and departure boards above the way to the trains had been digitized and now showed up in orange, just like every other station by now I imagine, replacing the old black and white analogue boards which would announce, in a burst of sinuous clattering, any newly arrived train or any platform changes, as the mechanism rifled through the numbers and letters until it came to a sudden stop when it came upon the right name, and the correct time. Indeed, in those days, you could afford to look around and up at the ceiling and at all the shop and café signs, because everyone turned their heads simultaneously when they heard that sound which was like the shuffling of cards, to see whether information about their train was now being displayed. What beguiled and astounded me every time, though, was that after any given train left, the board for that particular train would go backwards, running through the letters and numbers and times in reverse, going back, back, back, until it reached nothingness and the board would be black once more, almost as if these boards had the ability to turn back time itself, cancelling out all the delays and the waiting, and returning to the empty, blank board of that morning before all the travelers appeared and vanished in their turn. As I turned my gaze once more to the entrance of Euston station, preparing to make my exit at last, I wondered whether they had done away with the old analogue boards in order to dispel that deceptive and spectral effect, bringing in the digital boards instead, on which names and times could be changed in the blink of an eye without running through all the tiles; was it to prevent all those travelers from being deceived into thinking, and even believing, just for a moment in the midst of their day off or their workday, that it was possible to return unsullied once more to that morning or to the day before, or even further back in the past?

When I reached the hotel I dropped my bags in my room, noticing that there was a painting of the façade of the Duomo in Florence, in green and white, hanging above the bed, and I was reminded of that piece of unidentified music I'd heard in the square in front of the Palazzo Vecchio, and I failed to get rid of it properly from my mind for the whole of my stay in London that weekend. I took the tube to Elephant & Castle in order to visit the Imperial War Museum, and I spent quite some time there looking at the planes and enormous tanks in the main hall, and then in the galleries upstairs, where there were endless glass cupboards and panels and pictures and letters and objects all chronicling the different experiences of people in a whole range of different wars and conflicts; then I ventured downstairs to the floor beneath the main hall, to visit the *Trench Experience.* Here you could step inside, through a door in a corridor of quite unremarkable appearance, and immediately you would be in a trench somewhere in eastern France or Belgium, in the dead of night. On the right as you went in was a shelter for an officer, and indeed there was an officer made of plastic or wax installed there, holding a phone to his ear, and you could hear him trying to connect with another regiment further down the front line, and then the phone line was cut off by an explosion, breaking his connection, and then the light would go out on him. If you stayed there long enough, the light would come on again and the same conversation would be played again, before the poor officer would once again lose the connection, and thus he remained, holding the same never-ending phone conversation day after day but never succeeding in getting the information that he needed. After this you would continue onwards through the real trench as it would have been at the front, with the stars glittering down from the ceiling above.

I was reminded, as I walked through this trench the top of which I couldn't see over, of an area of trenches near the Iser canal in Belgium which had been preserved, an area which stretched as far as a child's eyes could see, a grey scar on the brown, waste land. I had been transfixed by those trenches, and especially by the sandbags piled up on both sides of me, rising high above my head, forming the walls of the trench, but then I reached out my hand and touched one of the bags and realized as I touched its hard coldness that it was a cement mould in the shape of a sandbag, and though it was so realistic that the pattern of the sacking was to be seen on the cement the magic was gone for me and I felt quite disenchanted. Much more satisfactory from my point of view was the exhibition in Hill 62, where I spent hours gazing at the guns, shells, bullets, and various other bits of kit and weaponry that had been retrieved from the battlefields and gathered in glass cases, and also at the sepia photographs of battle-fields, and mud and trenches which you had to look at through little viewers, encased in wooden frames. One picture especially is seared on my memory, a picture of a horse that had been torn to bits and flung by the force of the explosion so that it hung in pieces from the highest branches of a nearby tree; I must have seen so many pictures of dead men's bodies half buried in the mud that this horse, which appeared suddenly somewhere in the midst of those pictures, seemed so different and so pitiful that it made much more of an impression on my young mind than all those dismembered human arms and legs.

At length I gave in to the rest of the family, who were already fed up, weary and keen to leave this morbid but astonishing museum, so we stepped out into trenches which were completely different from those near the Iser canal because their walls were made of corrugated iron, and because underfoot was not clean cement but actual mud, a thin and relatively inoffensive layer of mud admittedly, but mud all the same, and seeing the print of my own shoe in the mud as I walked back and forth over the duckboards through the undulations of the trenches gave me a thrill such as I never experienced in the straight, neat trenches of the Iser canal. There's a picture of me, later on, when I was about ten or eleven, standing outside the museum's café on the brink of a hole made by a shell or bomb, and I'm pointing at it, and the expression on my face is uncertain, as if I don't know whether I should be smiling or not.

There was no mud in the *Trench Experience* in the Imperial War Museum in London, but there were plastic or wax soldiers, one over there lying down in a kind of bay or alcove in the trench wall, rummaging through his food tin and writing a letter home, another using his periscope to look over the top of the sandbags opposite, and there was another periscope beside him inviting the curious visitor to do the same as him and to look, over the barrenness and barbed wire of no-man's-land, towards the light of a cigarette in the distance, where a careless German soldier was enjoying a smoke. There was a strange smell coming from somewhere, too, a smell both damp and sharp, almost peppery, and I was puzzled because I couldn't decide whether this smell was meant to convey the smell of the food from the nearby soldier's tin, or the smell of piss or of rats, or the general rotten smell of the trenches. Considering how few other visitors I had come across in the upstairs galleries, I was also struck by the busyness of these particular trenches as a large number of visitors brushed quite hastily past me and out through a door at the farther end, where the peppery smell still lingered for some yards down the corridor.

It was to this exhibition, and to another similar one at the far end of the basement, the *Blitz Experience*, where a group of people were led out from some kind of shelter, after they had heard and felt the bombs falling outside, into a street in the East End, to see the destruction everywhere, yes, it was to these exhibitions that the visitors flocked, in their eagerness to re-live these experiences, rather than to look at an exhibition of disconnected, untouchable objects in a glass cabinet. To my own mind there came a mixture of sensations – a narrow strip of bright, cold stars and the smell of damp earth – but then other images arrived to displace those. Yellow lights hanging from low roofs, the sound of footsteps echoing along corridors and the metallic clunk of steel doors shutting somewhere, and then the smell of camphor and disinfectant, tins of food and pint glasses with handles, cobbled streets and dark pubs in narrow streets, and songs about Tipperary and the white cliffs of Dover. And then I was in the back of the car in Dover with the family on a grey morning in August, the car already warming up, and all of us racking our brains trying to remember the words of the Vera Lynn song about the blue birds.

After this memorable if ersatz experience, I went back up the stairs, in search of a corner or a cabinet or a panel which would tell me about the campaigns of the Second World War in Syria. I wandered around for quite a while, up and down stairs, in dark corners and past panels about the Blitz, Vietnam, the Boer wars, the siege of Stalingrad, before finding myself in a large, new, utterly harrowing exhibition about the Holocaust, where I was the only visitor for the whole time I was there, until I began to feel quite fearful on account of the terrifying nature of the pictures and film reels being projected on the walls around me, appearing gigantic, and the dim lighting of the entire exhibition, and the endless lists, name after name, of Jews, gay people, Roma and the thousands of others who had been exterminated, until I felt overcome with giddiness and nausea, surrounded as I was by the faces and the names and the huts and the chimneys and the naked bodies swirling around, and I had to head immediately for the exit and find a bench, near the white doors of the toilets in a corridor which ran along the edge of the building, in order to rest and come to my senses. As I sat there I recalled that there had been a much smaller and more traditional exhibition there in former times when my father and I had visited, separately from the rest of the family, ignoring the warning sign at the entrance that this department was not suitable for anyone under the age of fifteen years, but my father had thought me mature enough, if such a thing as being mature enough existed, in the face of such atrocities, and so I went with him, holding on tightly to his hand. At that time there were only a few pictures and videos to be seen amongst the panels, very different from the multi-media experience that I had just been through, and I remember one video in particular, lasting about thirty seconds and playing on a loop, showing a gigantic heap of naked, skeletal bodies that had been thrown on top of one another outside a wooden hut, and then a JCB appearing from somewhere to push these bodies roughly into a large open pit which had been dug for that purpose. The way in which these bodies had been thrown seemed so surreal and so unlike any body that I had ever seen, and it was hard to make out properly, somehow, whether these body parts were legs or arms or what that lay upon one another higgledy-piggledy, until they fell over each other into the pit in this shaky film; the scene struck me as strange and almost comic, like the pictures of those bodies in Hill 62, so much so that I even let out a sudden laugh before realizing, young as I was, that laughter in the face of such a scene was repugnant.

I remember the shame I felt then; indeed I'm blushing now just remembering it, seeing that the only other person in the exhibition at the time had turned, on hearing the laugh, to stare at me and tut-tut. My father had not heard my laugh, or at least he pretended not to have heard, nor did he notice the reaction of the other visitor, but I was soon tugging at his sleeve to urge him to leave, so that we could rejoin my mother and the rest of the family, who were by now outside the museum in the sunshine, far far away from that dark exhibition, and my brother and sister were playing a game which involved climbing up on the cannon which stood defiantly outside the museum's neoclassical façade. By now, as I sat outside the toilets on the fourth floor, I felt steady enough to venture to stand up, and keeping the memory of the sunshine in my mind I made my way slowly, keeping hold of the handrail, down the stairs and out into a grey, windy day which nevertheless seemed, on emerging from the murky bowels of the museum, like one of the brightest of Spring days. I heard that they closed the museum shortly after my visit, in order to refurbish it in time for the celebration-commemoration of 2014, and that neither the *Trench Experience* nor the *Blitz Experience* had actually survived the transformation. It's strange to think that that trench now only exists in my memory, as well as in a picture or two, just as the real trenches came to exist only in the memories of fewer and fewer old men until they all, one by one, died.

In the afternoon I walked around the City, starting at Aldwych and making my way towards the Tower, and then following the river westwards to Monument, before working my way back to the centre, until I reached Leadenhall market. Since it was a weekend, the City was unnaturally quiet, the streets where the bankers and traders would be milling about in during the week so empty that there was no need for me to look both ways before crossing the road; the regular commandments painted on the road to 'Look Right' and 'Look Left' were never more unnecessary. Leadenhall, which has been the site of a market of some sort or another since at least the fourteenth century, was no different, and was, if anything, even quieter, because it was hidden away from the main road, behind a skyscraper or two, and the mock-Victorian shops, with their painted signs instead of the usual neon ones, seemed dark and dusty, as if the owners and customers had left them decades before and as if no-one had dared disturb the place until I came across them on my wanderings, and my footsteps on the cobblestones echoed around the high, decorated, purple vaults of the green and cream and maroon and blue-coloured ceiling.

On the corner of one of the entrances to the market a part of the street was closed off with temporary wooden boards, and on one of these boards was an information panel explaining what was behind the boards. The panel explained that the excavation work which was being undertaken there was extremely important, for Leadenhall market stood on a site which had once been the centre, and indeed the heart, of the Roman town of Londinium, and that it had been here, on this corner, that the forum and market of that Roman settlement had led to the Basilica, which had been such an enormous building at the time that it could be seen from miles away, and certainly from every part of the town itself. Between the oppressive silence of the market and the darkness of the shops and the stillness of the counters and tables, and the feeling that I was trespassing on more than one past as I stood in this place, I left it and wandered fairly aimlessly on through the streets of the city, steering a reasonably convoluted path towards the Royal Exchange and the Bank, and beyond that towards Saint Paul's Cathedral.

Sometimes the wind would whirl up fiercely to sweep its way through the broad streets, scattering the dust of the week over my hair, and this made me notice the sudden and surprising difference between some of the narrowest and windiest little streets and the wide, straight avenues that they led to now and again. My attention was also taken by the way that the architectural style shifted from one street to the next, ranging from the more or less medieval to the neoclassical, and then to the ugly concrete heaps or worse still those buildings that looked as if they were made entirely of glass. Many buildings were arranged in layers which diminished as they rose higher, as if they were emulating staircases or, on closer inspection, perhaps were post-war pastiches of Art Deco, and it struck me then that that was precisely what accounted for this strange variety of architectural styles, since some buildings had survived the bombardments of the Blitz and others had been razed to the ground. Londoners had then set to with a will to rebuild the old halls, taller and stronger and more magnificent, so that I realized that when I looked at these buildings I was therefore in a manner of speaking looking at the sites and locations of the bombing. Wherever there was the most pompous and presumptuous-looking building, that too was the site of the worst destruction, and so I was, as I walked through the city, seeing the devastation as if I were looking at the negative of an old film, the white appearing black, and the black, white.

After buying a sandwich in the crypt of Saint Paul's Cathedral, I made the most of the opportunity to take a look at a model of the forum and the Basilica I had intruded upon so insolently just a couple of hours before, a model which was in the Museum of London quite close by. As I walked over to the museum through another quiet subway, it felt as if the building, like a cornered animal, was attempting to make itself look bigger in order to frighten me, because of the way in which the entrance was raised above the level of the street. On this upper level, the museum was connected by means of a series of cement avenues, which formed straight lines edged with hidden concrete gardens, with the labyrinthine complex of the Barbican, a mish-mash of entertainment centres and flats which had been built above the city streets in the sixties so that the putative inhabitants need not set foot on the earth practically from morning till night, and which was, I believed, the apotheosis of that building project which I had seen evidence of throughout the afternoon. However, the many entrances of the Barbican, and the various different levels, meant that both visitors and residents had depended for years on the painted marks and lines on the floors of the centre to help them find their way around the labyrinth, and I wondered whether these people had suffered too from a kind of vertigo or light-headedness as a result of being so far away from any solid ground for so long, like the mountain-dwellers years ago, feeling somehow safer here in their high places.

As I walked around the museum, which started on the top floor with the Romans, giving us a glimpse through glass of the old Roman wall that was underneath us outside, and then moved on chronologically as the visitor passed on down through the levels, I was still thinking about those poor souls on the Barbican, going up and up all the time, or even being shoved upwards, and then I remembered the attraction that we as children used to love to visit when we came to London years ago. The name of the attraction was the Tower Hill Pageant, and after paying to get in one was escorted in the lift down to the bowels of the earth and one would then be taken in a little carriage on a ride through the history of the river Thames, which took the form of a series of *tableaux* and models, from the earliest dwellings to the Romans, through the Plague years (where you would be surrounded by an unpleasant smell, not dissimilar to the smell in the *Trench Experience*), before passing the narrow streets of the city, a model of a red-cheeked man pissing in an alley, the Great Fire, and coffee shops...

The thing which I found most terrifying, though, was the lift that took you down to this carriage, because one of its walls was made of glass, and so you could watch yourself descend through the earth, through the strata of the city itself, and while that was happening, a red LED panel above the door would be counting back through the years, from 199- to such and such a year before Christ, with the result that you were convinced that you were not only travelling through the earth but back through time itself. As I thought of these things I was struck by just how much history was encapsulated in one city, history which had been hidden and left in layer after layer, and yet in spite of all the efforts to build, and to construct, and to rise up, leaving this history beneath, everyone eventually groped their way back down, whether that was by descending the stairs to the Churchill War Rooms or the London Dungeons, or by visiting the Tower Hill Pageant or taking the daily commute on the tube; yes, it was back to the bowels of their own history that Londoners were drawn every day, while the high, windy avenues of the Barbican remained deserted.

The next day I travelled from my hotel in the city centre to Kew, in order to visit the National Archives there, only to find, when I arrived, that the building, like so many hairdressers, was closed on Mondays. I had decided that I would visit the place in person after reading an anonymous review on the web which complained that the reviewer had paid forty pounds to get a copy of the documents he wanted sent to him, but that the documents had failed to arrive, and the online account which the poor fellow had created to order the papers had disappeared by the time he returned to the website, leaving no record that he had ever paid his money and placed his order, and though he had contacted them many times he had never received anything but automatic emails in return. As I stood in front of the building that day, with nobody in sight and all the windows in darkness, I felt for a minute as if I were back in Leadenhall market, and that not a single creature had set foot in this place for some years, and that the archives didn't exist at all any more, if they ever had existed at all.

The next day, however, was sunny and I repeated the half-hour journey by tube, to find the place utterly transformed, full of life and threatening even to appear welcoming, with the sun beating down on the concrete building, turning the straight lines of the cement golden, almost, and illuminating even the brownish black squares of the windows. Nevertheless, my researches in the Archives that day proved comparatively fruitless, and in the tube station waiting for a train to take me back to the centre, I decided for some reason not to get on the first train which thundered out of the tunnel into the light of the platform but rather to wait for the next, because, so I rationalized later, of some curiosity which made me want to see what the Underground platform would be like after the bustle of departure. The few travelers dashed for the carriages, the train doors closed leaving me outside, and with a low humming which gradually grew louder, the train left the station behind, drawing the wind into the tunnel after it like someone breathing in.

I watched the dust and dirt swirling about before settling down once more, and I listened to the few leaves near the stairs whirling, rustling, and then lying still. The footsteps of the one or two travelers who had got off the train echoed as they made their way to the exit, and there was one other person in a long coat standing at the other end of the platform. That person coughed, and my gaze caught his as both of us looked at the information board from time to time, watching the remaining time tick away, before the next train thundered its way towards us. The rats down on the track started to scrut once more, and it felt as if the station, which had taken a breath and held it in as the train left, was now beginning to breathe again. I myself felt the same, somehow or other, as I tried to trace and track the Second World War through this city, while it persisted in slipping away from me whenever I caught hold of it. The war in all its horror had thundered through the world, and the world had held its breath. Now we who were left behind on the platform were able to start breathing again, and coughing, and listening to the dust settle, but at the same time we knew that the travelers in those carriages were racing further and further away from us, and that they would soon be at the farthest reaches of the city, at the most distant edge, and that we needed to gather every particle of dust before they reached the ground again. When the next train arrived I did not hesitate but got on it at once and found a seat.

Late that afternoon before catching the train home I came up from the depths of the Underground into Marble Arch station, crossed the road towards Speakers' Corner, and then wound my way through Hyde Park towards the south-eastern corner. A strong breeze blew up, sweeping over the cars and along the broad lanes of the road, making the branches of the trees creak. Various city cyclists and joggers speeded past me, and seeing the joggers in their T-shirts and lycra made me wrap my coat more tightly around me and turn my collar up. When I reached the corner I crossed the road and made my way to a rather pathetic-looking memorial which stood next to a neater, more modern memorial, which I later discovered had been erected in 2003 to commemorate the loss of Australian soldiers in the two world wars. The curved, clean, slate-grey lines of this enormous memorial was very different from the one I had come to see, namely the memorial to the Royal Artillery which was first unveiled in 1925, though it was added to after the Second World War. This monument was characterized by straight, sharp lines and angles, and it rose up perpendicularly with a model of a Howitzer gun at its pinnacle. Four bronze soldiers stood around the gun, and on the sides of the monument were carved a number of battle scenes. These depictions made no effort, unlike so many other memorials, to hide or to romanticize or to create a heroic ideal out of war, but rather were terrifyingly realistic, so much so that they seemed almost brutal in their rawness. There was, however, a layer of some kind of moss or algae rapidly growing over the monument, turning its white stone to a slimy green, and the fact that the memorial was in dire need of a thorough cleaning had a twofold effect on me. Firstly, it lent a trace of irony to the inscription on one side of the memorial which declared 'Their Glory Will Abide For Ever', but in addition to that, somehow or other the moss succeeded in softening the sharpness and hardness of the original design to an extent so that the whole thing felt, obscurely, more appropriate. Like the black veil over the Eisteddfod Chair in 1917, this growth covered the sharp cruelty of its stark whiteness and prevented it from dazzling my eyes too brutally. I moved on then to look at the plaques that were added after the Second World War, and under the motto *Ubique,* the meaning of which I did not know, though I naturally guessed that it was Latin, was a list of places from the four points of the compass. The list read like a mixture of neighboring countries and far-flung, exotic, unknown ones: France, Belgium, the Netherlands, Norway, Iceland, Greece, Crete, the Dodecanese, Malta, Gibraltar, Cyprus, Palestine, Jordan, Syria, Iraq, Persia, Aden, Abyssinia, Somaliland, Eritrea, Sudan, Madagascar, Egypt, Libya, Tunisia, Algeria, Sicily, Italy, Yugoslavia, India, Ceylon, Burma, Malaya, Singapore, Sumatra, Java, Hong Kong, and lastly, and perhaps the most terrifyingly romantic of them all, 'The High Seas'. I realized that many of these countries no longer existed, or at least that they did not have the same names, and as for the rest, many of them were familiar to me because conflict of some sort was still going on there today.

*

Although I managed to get hold of only a limited amount of information, after all, from the diaries of the various regiments in the National Archives at Kew, I had also been in touch by email with an expert on the 60th Field Regiment of the Royal Artillery, and when I got back home from London there was a parcel awaiting me, and inside it was a book on the history of the regiment, along with a short note which eagerly informed me that this was the only regiment that could claim to have fought in every main theatre, and against every enemy, during the Second World War, and that therefore the motto on their badge, *Ubique*, meaning 'everywhere' in Latin, was exceptionally appropriate in their case. That solved the puzzle of the memorial, then, and it gradually dawned on me that the list of places I read on the memorial was a list of all the territories in which the Royal Artillery had fought. Indeed, the gentleman scholar indicated, it would be possible to add to this *Ubique*, for they were, thanks to their having fought in every main theatre of war, also, of course, *Unique*. So small, then, had John's role been, so insignificant had the suffering of my family been, when one considered that 29,924 members of the Royal Artillery had been killed in the Second World War, and when one considered that many continued to fight, *Ubique*, in these places until the present day.

A strong smell of pipe smoke came off the pages of the book as I read that the regiment had initially, on the outbreak of war, been sent to Trawsfynydd for training, a coincidence perhaps in view of the fact that the vast majority of them were a bunch of lads from Lincolnshire and that John, who was, of course, by then living in Manchester, had been assigned to the regiment at random like every other soldier who enlisted after war broke out. The men then crossed the channel to France, before being driven back by the German offensive and retreating once more to England. I wasn't sure when exactly John enlisted but I did know, from the letters, that he was certainly with the regiment when they embarked on the *Scythia* en route to Iraq. The crew of the *Scythia* had been forced to take additional soldiers on board because another ship, the *Pasteur*, refused point blank to set sail, and so conditions were quite crowded for everyone on deck, with not enough hammocks to go round, let alone beds. But after some delay, according to this book, the *Scythia* set sail from Gourock near Glasgow out into the firth of Clyde on the 8th of February 1941, with John among those on board, before a convoy of about thirty other ships joined her out at sea. Out on the Atlantic, stormy weather meant that a number of the men could scarcely get up from their beds for days on end, and indeed some of the officers had started to lose their tempers with the poor creatures since all these cases of seasickness were in their view a sign of weakness. But before long the lads managed to begin to set about entertaining themselves, by means of cinemas and choirs, tug-of-war contests and tombolas, and indeed the food on board the *Scythia* was so bad that some of the men felt that the relentless seasickness was a blessing in disguise, since it meant that they did not have to set foot in the dining room. To those who were still on their feet, and were brave enough to venture in there, the only things available to eat day after day were tinned rabbit, ancient herrings, and sago.

In the midst of this, some ships were leaving the convoy, others were joining, and the entire fleet steering a zig-zag course over the Atlantic as the ocean fell calm, and the weather improved with every day that passed. Rather awkwardly and shyly did the crew of the *Scythia* don their tropical white tunics for the first time, according to the author of this volume, but before long the sea was a most brilliant blue and the men were starting to spot dolphins and sharks regularly, and at night watching the rest of the convoy ploughing its way through the water in the moonlight was a memorable sight. By March the *Scythia* had reached Sierra Leone, and in Freetown the men enjoyed being entertained by the arc-lit Royal Marines band on board ship, for there was no blackout there, and they played rather mean tricks on the native people who brought them food in their small boats, refusing to pay them and instead filling their boats with water from hosepipes. Soon after, the ship crossed the equator, and both the Northern Star and the Southern Cross were to be seen clearly in the skies above.

I tried to imagine John in the midst of all this, imagining him full of amazement at the clear, starry night sky and I wondered whether he was comparing these strange constellations with those familiar ones that shone above Canol Arren, or how long he could really concentrate, in the debilitating heat, on the various lectures on first aid, gas attacks, semaphore lessons, even the question and answer sessions about the handling of guns, but though I searched for him on the deck, I failed to find him among all the white tunics and bare backs, and I could not even begin to comprehend either the tenor of his thoughts or his feelings. Then the *Scythia* sailed past Cape Town, in more of a hurry because water supplies were getting low, but then the sea turned rough again after rounding the Cape of Good Hope, and men were disembarking from time to time at various ports to go to their appointed stations, some to Southern Rhodesia and others to Durban. The lads of the 60th spent six memorable days in Durban, being regaled with free drinks and having guided tours of the clean city with its broad avenues, and on the last Saturday, after they paraded through the city which looked as if all its citizens had come out to cheer them, there was a concert in the city hall in their honour, before the ship weighed anchor once more at the start of April, loaded with gifts of grapes, apples, pineapples, and magazines, which the lads' new friends had given them.

I read that as they neared the equator once more the sweltering heat returned again, and sometime in that period the regiment's monkey was lost because no-one had the energy to go and look for him. For some reason this little story seemed strangely familiar, but I couldn't for the life of me remember where I'd heard a story similar to this one before, until I bumped into a friend, Dafydd Timothy, on the Eisteddfod field a few months later. I remembered straight away then about the story that he had told me of his father, Owen, who had been a member of the medical corps on the same sea journey as Uncle John. However, Owen D. Timothy had taken the journey a year before my Uncle John, and he had added the detail that the monkey had been lost overboard. His diaries are full of colourful little details, and though there are not many of them, there's a sort of magic about them which somehow means we can taste that mango with him for the first time in Freetown, or see the native people crowding around the ships in their little boats, or watch the moon rising behind the trees and hills. The bare facts of that day, a Saturday in August 1940, are recorded like this in his diary:

> Monkeys, snakes bought by some chaps; 1 shirt for a monkey – went wild, some chaps bitten – Cpl. Cox. One ran up to top of mast. Dark at 7 pm. One monkey flung overboard.

Though there was a gap of a year between the two events, I felt that Uncle John's experiences on his sea voyage became much more vivid and colourful to me when I read such details, or that I was myself hearing the story in stereo, from two different perspectives, which were not entirely in accord with each other, like the sound of a gramophone in an empty railway station, and this feeling made the picture expand and reverberate like an echo. In the course of this voyage, as he watched the sun set on the equator, Owen Timothy was moved to compose a lovely poem about that sunset a few days after the diary entry above. But the poem of his which stays with me most is 'Their Creation', which was written in Calais in May 1940, before the sea journey, when he came across a dead soldier in a trench, whom he described as having fallen

Like a flower not fully open
Before it had a chance to blossom
Wilting in the afternoon sun.

The entries in Owen D. Timothy's diary, as transcribed by his son Dafydd up to this point, come to an end in September 1940, but I found out that he later went on to Syria, and he had served in Damascus during the battle for possession of the city. I did not venture or dare to ask Dafydd when exactly he had been there, nor did I ask for his diary entries while he was there looking at the fallen, nor did I ask whether he had written a poem similar to the one above about the poor soldier in Calais. The story of the sea voyage and the monkeys was still playing in stereo in my head, and suddenly it was far too easy to believe in things like fate and coincidence to dare ask any further questions.

This feeling was exacerbated later by the knowledge that the author I had been in contact with was not the person who told this story in the first-person in the book. In the preface, the second author explained how he had collaborated with the first author to bring this volume out, but that the first author, just as the last draft of the book was completed, had been struck down by illness. He had pulled the leg of his friend, neighbour and collaborator, saying that they would have to hurry or he would have pegged it before the book was published, and indeed within a few days he did indeed die. Throughout my reading of the book, then, I was aware that this voice, too, was as it were coming from beyond the grave, and there was no way of my contacting him any more, to ask him whether he had known my grandfather's brother, whether he had perhaps encountered him as he crossed the deck to go for a shave one morning. I knew that the papers were full these days of stories about somebody or other who had served or simply lived through the war, but had passed away, and many of the stories had died with them, and we would at some point reach the stage when there was no longer anybody left alive who could remember the conflict, the rationing, the digging, the shooting, so that I felt as if I were standing on that platform in Kew once again, and the last train of the day had left without me.

They didn't cross the equator again on their way up the other side until Good Friday, and soon after that the Royal Navy's guiding vessel left the *Scythia* to make her own way over the Indian Ocean and then through the Red Sea, until they reached the port of Tewfik, where the soldiers got their first taste of the intense cold of a desert night, and to learn that the war itself had been developing and changing rapidly while the lads had been suffering the oppressive heat on board their ship; the Italians had incurred Hitler's rage by attacking Greece, and the Allies, eventually,

had got the upper hand there. But the most griev-
ous problem was in Iraq, where the new Regent,
Rashid Ali, had broken the fragile peace with Britain and was threatening to expel all Britons from the
country. After some days of habituating themselves
to living in the desert, watching a film outdoors in
their shirtsleeves, and then having to put on heavy
overcoats halfway through because the sun had set,
and through it all trying to keep the blasted insects
at bay, the call came for them to go to Iraq, and it
was battery number 237 that went first because battery 239, John's battery, was not yet ready. But soon
after they followed their comrades through the Suez
Canal, over the Sinai desert to Palestine. Because the
author of the book was a member of battery 237, the
story in this chapter broadens out to such an extent
that it loses sight of John to all intents, and indeed at
this point I searched the index for his name, finding
that it wasn't there, and that made me realize once
again how small his part had been in the history of
the regiment, not to mention the war as a whole.

However, I learned that the British campaign
against the new Regent had been successful, and
that Baghdad had been retaken, after they had jour-
neyed through Jordan, crossed the desert and reached
Iraq, and some of the names there, such as Falluja
and Basra, were familiar to me because of the much
more recent war there. Though the Iraqi soldiers
received some support from the Italians, Rashid Ali
the Regent fled to Iran within a few days, allowing

the regiment to march into the centre of the city, to be welcomed there in pomp and circumstance by the British Ambassador. There was something uncanny about the way in which it seemed to me that history was repeating itself, or at least that this campaign had been foreshadowing, within the same territory, the British-American campaign at the start of the twenty-first century and indeed, as was suggested in this book, that it was fought for the same reasons, closely connected with the country's oil supplies. When I saw in the book a photograph of one of the army jeeps crossing a canal in the desert, I realized that there was nothing in that black and white picture, which was slightly blurry on account of the intense heat of the sun on the bridge, the vehicle, and the canal, nothing that could testify with any certainty as to whether it was taken in 1941 or in 2003.

Up to now, the whole thing sounded like a bit of an exuberant adventure. John, my grandfather's brother, had seen and experienced so much, had had a thoroughgoing adventure, before he met his death, so that I, though I knew of that heartbreaking ending, in some strange way felt envious of him, and of the chance that he took, to such an extent that I identified, for the first time actually, with those ubiquitous army advertisements urging you to join up and promising that you would then get the chance to see the world. I was often tempted to feel a certain amount of envy towards soldiers, whether they were of the present day or those who were called upon, in the flower of their days as it were, to serve. There was a kind of gamble associated with soldiering, because fundamentally and at the base of everything was the real and present danger of getting yourself killed, but on the other hand there was also that unmistakeable spirit of adventure, and excitement, and of seeing the world, and indeed the possibility that the experience would change your worldview completely.

I thought about individuals like Frantz Fanon, the anti-colonial thinker, who had racist atrocities perpetrated against him by the Vichy French during the war and had been influenced by those experiences for the rest of his life. Often amidst the monotony and inescapable restrictions of my daily life and work would come the desire, the fantasy even, that some big, old-fashioned war would break out and I would be forced to go away and fight. Such a departure would be a compulsory uprooting, in which I would be posted to a remote city or a barren desert, to Trieste like James Morris or Dar-es-Salaam like Roald Dahl, or somewhere distant of that ilk at the very edges of Empire, and invariably 'in the dying days of the war'. Tell me, is there a more romantic phrase than this amid the great riches of the English language, 'the dying days of the war'? Of course there would be a heartbroken girl in some cottage somewhere waiting for me, darning socks and biting her nails to the quick as she listened to the ticking of the clock and gazed soulfully through the window, and I would in due course be overcome by the romance and tragedy of it all.

Of course that would be to use the compulsion and duress of war, to use the heroic, brave arena of that, ironically enough, to make up for my own cowardice. It is cowardice, a feeling of impotence, the unconquerable burden of having to make choices in the midst of a world laden with a plethora of choices and decisions, that has meant that I am to this very day sitting and staring at a blank screen trying to write, or failing to concentrate on a paragraph in a book, rather than jettisoning all this work, all the rituals of relations and acquaintances, all the bonds of family and society and nation and picking up my knapsack to journey to the other side of the world once again. It was because of this that I was envious of Uncle John, of Cynan,[1] of Churchill and of Frantz Fanon. They had no choice but to stand up and be counted, to take that risk, and in the case of my Uncle John, to lose the gamble, but in the case of Churchill, or Saunders Lewis, it gave them that astonishing mixture of a sense of adventure and rash patriotism that drove them on to lead, to display bravery, and to make their most defiant declarations. In the case of Fanon the experience influenced his worldview and politics so completely that it meant that, even bearing in mind the fact that he died suddenly at the age of thirty-six, his writing would be acknowledged as among the most important voices of protest against the greed of imperialism and

[1] Albert Evans Jones, the Welsh poet and later Archdruid who served in Salonika during the First World War and later won the crown for his ode *Mab y Bwthyn*, a semi-autobiographical account of the conflict and its aftermath.

colonialism. Because of these things I was envious of them, almost against my own will and instinct, that war, in addition to killing men, also made men.

And I suspect, too, that this envy went deeper than just that incredible sea voyage, but that it also extended to that camp in Egypt and the journey to Iraq, even, and perhaps went as far as that battle in Syria, for John had had an opportunity that I had never had, and that I never would, probably, namely this opportunity to see and experience real suffering, and to see and experience in reality what it meant to face danger, lethal danger, and had therefore had the opportunity to behave like a hero. It was even more peculiar, however, to turn the page in the history of the regiment and find, in the chapter about the Syria campaign, that it had not been against the Germans that they were fighting, for all John's talk in his letters about 'Jerry', but rather the French. I couldn't comprehend, when I saw the title of the chapter, Fighting the French, what the author was referring to, and I thought for a moment that he had made a serious error, but when I read it, I found that he too was asking 'Who on earth would have thought that we would find ourselves fighting against the French?', and I understood that that was precisely what they had been doing there.

In the course of the campaign against Iraq, the British found themselves under attack by Messerschmitt aeroplanes, which could not have come from anywhere other than Syria, a country under French rule that was supposed to be neutral, but the French there were true to the Vichy government, the one that had agreed to ally itself with the Germans. The regiment was therefore sent, without more ado, to Syria, along with a group of Australians, some Frenchmen from the other side, and a bunch of foot-soldiers from India. They were led back on a three-day march through the desert by Glubb Pasha and his Bedouins, who were called 'Glubb's Girls' by the British on account of their draped clothing and long hair. The aim then was to mount a three-pronged attack on Damascus, but it's clear that the French fought back against this motley crew much more ferociously than had been expected, and the main problem was the planes, which would appear out of nowhere firing on the troops below and dropping bombs, and the foot-soldiers in the midst of the desert heat had nowhere to shelter from either the sun or the bullets. Several members of the company became unhinged during this period it seems, and when I read the account of one of them being taken away quietly to a hospital in Jerusalem, I felt it was possible to hear the note of envy in the voice of the author.

Yet again here, the place-names sounded remarkably familiar: Homs, Aleppo, ancient names which have been re-inscribed again with a myriad of new, terrifying meanings. And yet, though the book and the regimental diaries I found in the Archives in Kew were full of technical details and traced the troops' every movement, John is as it were lost in the midst of it all; it was like trying to distinguish a single particle of a signal in the middle of a screenful of static. It was only when I read the account of the author and his battery approaching Damascus on the tenth of July, and of his celebrating his twenty-first birthday, like John, in mid-August, that I realized that it was already too late, that John was as it were in another book somewhere else, wounded, and by that time already dead, and that the history of the campaign had already moved on without him. That *Ubique* had sounded so straightforward when I first read it above the list on the memorial, but now I saw the enormity of what some of the lads, those men, had seen and faced in a period of just five years, for they had in due course conquered Syria, and had left the dead behind them in their new graves, while they moved on to another adventure in Egypt, India, Burma. I had not yet reached a third of the way through the book.

I had hoped that reading these things would have brought me somehow closer to Uncle John. From one point of view, I had learned a great deal more about the movements of the regiment, their adventurous voyage around the Cape of Good Hope, and the small details such as the story of the monkey had afforded me some kind of connection, and had made the whole thing come a little more alive. The CO, too, sounded like a bit of a character, with his stammer and the pompous manner in which he told off the lads, and yet there was something in the way they called him 'Uncle Joe', and the strangely familiar and comforting sound of that nickname, that succeeded in confusing the usual preconceptions about the harsh nature of the relationship between officers and soldiers, and in giving the slightest of hints to the reader of the human scale of it all. But I felt John's absence on every page, his distance, and that feeling was encapsulated in the fact that I searched long and carefully through every photograph in the book, studying every face meticulously, narrowing my eyes and turning the book every which way, hoping in that way perhaps to see John's face coming into view between the faces of two of his friends, materializing, coming into being in front of my eyes, and being able to recognize him by the shape of his nose which was so like Auntie Olwen's, or the sweep of hair across his forehead which was uncannily like my grandfather's hair. But he didn't come, and so I did not derive the same enjoyment from this volume as I had from reading John's own letters, or the story of someone like Hedd Wyn, or even Anne Frank, distant and inchoate figures with whom I have no blood relation or personal link but who can make one feel, despite that, that their personalities, their humanity, leap from the page to meet the insignificant reader, as if they were walking towards someone from Trawsfynydd or Amsterdam.

My memories of my time with Cynon in Amsterdam, on our way between Munich and Belgium, are also more vague and blurry than my memories of other places we visited on our trip. It is quite possible that that is because of the café the two of us visited on our first night there, and as we were rather too eager to taste the delicacies that were set before us, we had devoted ourselves to smoke some things that we should not have smoked, so that I had, at one point, risen rather unsteadily to my feet to go to the toilet upstairs, and when I came out again had failed to remember the way back down. In the same way, perhaps, I was no longer able to remember the way down through the rest of the visit, but I also suspect that the fogginess is also to do with the fact that there's a gap of about four or five pages in my travel journal for that period; these pages are quite empty apart from the name, Amsterdam, and the note-to-self which directs me to my online blog and reminds me that I need to copy my entry there for the city into my journal. I had been putting that off for months and then forgot to do it completely, and by now, after a diligent search on the net, I found that the website has been deleted, and the blog lost forever. On the whole that is a relief because a number of the entries gave away my rather fragile mental state and the characteristic immaturity of a nineteen-year-old youth, and yet I do regret that I didn't succeed in motivating myself sufficiently to ensure that those words were recorded somewhere else too, just in case.

As I tried to remember our movements around Amsterdam I realized how dependent memory is on pictures and words to direct and prompt it, which made me wonder how much of the rest of the trip would be still vivid for me now if I hadn't taken so many pictures and had not written in my little journal ritualistically and almost without fail every evening or in the small hours of the morning. Indeed, as I sought in vain for the entry in an earlier journal, where I had added a section about an enjoyable evening I had spent with fellow-travellers in the Idiot café in St Petersburg, I read the following words of mine, which were written, clearly, in order to justify the unceremonious insertion of this isolated event into the middle of another narrative: 'Nothing incredible but I had to make a record of the evening so that it doesn't slip into oblivion', and when I read those words I thought they were a pretty accurate description of what, as far as I can tell, I'm doing in writing this book.

Although the entry on Amsterdam is indeed in oblivion the spirit of the place still remains, and I remember that I was somewhat thrown by the geographical layout of the city, all the canals like rings in a tree trunk or on the surface of water when a raindrop has fallen into it, radiating outwards and growing from the centre, but the main railway station, though it was called Amsterdam Central, was not actually quite in the centre, but situated some distance to the north and away from that which represented the central point of the city, and with its red bricks and its white decorations, it reminded me of a gingerbread house and therefore liable to crack and fall at any moment. I remember too that the actual centre did not appeal to me, and that the exciting and risqué nature of this area, which had been quite an eye-opener and an adventure for two little Welsh boys on the first night, simply appeared dirty, dishevelled and slightly seedy by morning, and in the light of that morning Cynon and I had emerged from the hovel which called itself a hostel where we were staying, rather red about the eyes but temporarily safe from the depredations of the rats which ran through its corridors; out into the street where the kebab cartons from last night still lay and were gathered in corners along with one or two stray condoms.

I think it was Cynon who suggested the trip on the boat, doing so perhaps as a sign or a suggestion that the long nights were at last beginning to defeat him, but both of us soon realized, as the boat ploughed onwards through the canals, that in our current state this trip had been a mistake, since the boat was built in such a way that we tourists could look out and marvel at the city's architecture, the tall, narrow houses painted in different colours, and their rows of identical windows, and the hook that projected from every house front because the only way of getting pieces of furniture into those constricted houses was by raising them on ropes threaded onto those hooks and then taking them in through the windows, but we meanwhile were sheltered from the elements. On this sweltering hot day, however, we weren't being protected from the elements but rather the transparent plastic covers were actually exacerbating the effects of the elements upon us, for the little boat had been turned into a greenhouse. To avoiding melting completely, the two of us alighted from the boat at the first possible stop, and that was, as it happened, in front of the *Anne Frank Huis*. I was keen to visit the house, and since Cynon had no objection, we both joined the queue that snaked around the corner and disappeared into the modern glass extension on the corner of the street where the entrance was.

Again, for some reason my memories of the interior of the house are extremely blurred, and that surprises me somewhat, for I remember now, as if I were outside myself and looking on, that the house was displayed in an exceptionally interesting and educational way. I remember more or less how the visitor was led through the different storeys of the house, where there were a number of exhibitions and films about the life of the family and the situation of the Jews in Amsterdam during the war, and there was even a miniature model of the secret annexe at the back of the house, set in front of the bookcase through which one stepped into that very annexe, as the little family itself would have had to do. I remember that bookcase clearly, but I can't for the life of me remember a single thing about the rooms I saw behind it after I stepped through, nor do I remember the feelings and emotions I experienced at the time, and to be honest it's almost easier for me to see myself and Cynon from afar, as if I were looking in on us wandering through that miniature model in the glass case, than to remember the small, bare kitchen, and the heavy beams that bent inwards and intruded upon the claustrophobic space, and the green-painted door- and window-frames, and the flowery wallpaper which has yellowed by now, and even the marks on that paper where the girls' father had traced their growth in ink.

It's a strange world these days when I can visit those places online, and see them clearly, in three dimensions, through the medium of an interactive website, and I can feel intense sympathy for dear Anne and her family, but I can't remember being moved to shed a single tear nor to feel much of anything when I visited that little annexe in the flesh. It may be that neither of us had woken up properly that morning, and we had also seen the effects of the

Second World War already lying like a shadow over so many European cities so that we were numbed in some way, numbed to the extent that the death of this little girl and her family could not make an indelible impression on us, and indeed by the time we came out again into the bright midday sun some minutes later, the whole experience was already beginning to fade. Perhaps I had not even come close to understanding, before then, how some people could cease to be considered as people under that shadow which was so far-reaching that it was easy to forget what sort of feeling it was not to be standing under it.

Some days later we had moved away from the hostel since Cynon had found a cheaper place for us, and my suspicions about any place that was cheaper than that dive of a hostel that we'd just escaped from were confirmed when we were met outside a block of flats by two shady-looking characters, who gave us the key and directed us up the stairs, before they disappeared for the rest of our stay in the city, and my first sight of the flat strengthened my negative impressions since there were various objects and bits and pieces scattered around the place, as if someone were still living there, or indeed as if someone had been living there until very recently but had left, or been forced to leave, in something of a hurry. It was only when I saw this contemporary scene, I realize now, that the meaning of what we had seen in the *Anne Frank Huis* started to make an impression on me, and yet at the time I don't believe I could have differentiated between the effect that had and the effect on us that the apparently constant travelling and drinking that the two of us had been doing over the previous weeks.

I made an effort to get over this latest wave of depression that engulfed me by catching a tram down to the docks, by myself, because I'd heard about a jazz evening that was going to be held at an arts centre down there, so I left Cynon drinking and watching football on the television in the flat. The building that housed the arts centre turned out to be a monstrous carbuncle of brutalist modern architecture, and I had to walk quite a long way along the edge of a motorway before I managed to get there at all. By the time I arrived, and had made my way up the stairs to the right floor, the evening was already well under way, in a proper theatre, which meant that if I wanted to watch and listen I would have to go in and cross in front of the stage in the middle of the performance, which would disturb everyone. This was utterly different from the idealised picture I had in my head of a cellar in a little tavern on a back street in the city centre, where the wooden tables and the low beams were hard to discern because of the smoke, and the music was coming from somewhere blurry at the other end of the room as well as from the bottle of wine in front of me, and so I went to a bar outside the theatre, at least managing to order a bottle of wine, at least, and stayed there getting drunk before returning to the flat and falling asleep next to Cynon, who was already fast asleep.

I woke up in the morning with quite a sharp pain in the small of my back, as well as a headache and a sore throat, and I was convinced, though Cynon swore that he couldn't see anything, that some kind of rash was developing on my legs. I couldn't get out of bed or move much, and though Cynon grumbled and tried to persuade me to come out and look for some breakfast, I was preparing myself for a long and painful illness which was in tune with my growing belief, which had got stronger as we moved through the continent, that I was not long for this world. However, the illness did not materialize, and my lethargy wore off before long, together with the rash and the headache, but it wasn't until our last morning, when we left the strange flat behind us and made our way towards the gingerbread house of the station and the next country, the next city, that I managed to rid myself of that sense of paralysis and get out of my bed.

PART 3

EASTER 2012

My research entailed my having to go and sift through some of the papers of W. B. Yeats which are kept in the National Library of Ireland in Dublin, and at Easter 2012, while I was free of my teaching responsibilities, I took advantage of the opportunity to go to the city and spend a week there. On a grey and windy Monday morning I left the car in the car park at the furthest end of the headland on the eastern side of the dock in Holyhead and waited for the shuttle bus to take me to the terminal, but after waiting for twenty minutes, seeing that I was the only living soul in the vicinity and that there was no sign of the bus, I decided to walk over despite the weight of my bags and books. The wind that whipped around every corner gave me an ominous premonition, and indeed I very nearly failed to keep down the stodgy Irish breakfast that I bought for an exorbitant price on the boat, especially the sausages which had been made with some kind of herbs that I'd never tasted before and that I wished never to taste again.

In order to keep my mind off the sea passage, I turned my attention to the television screen which was showing a news channel, and at that moment the presenter was explaining the work of the observers who had been sent to Syria to write a report on the situation there. The city of Homs was among the cities under the severest threat at the time, and reports were coming in daily of dozens of people being shot or found dead there, but NATO spokesmen were categorical in saying that they would not intervene in what was happening in the country, and at the same time some of the rebels were already presenting and broadcasting their vision for a new Syria to come after Assad. According to some reports, though the official observers could not confirm this, it was quite plain by now that the Syrian army was bombing and shelling locations indiscriminately, and civilians – men, women, and children – were being killed every day. In the meantime, the rebel army had taken Douma, on the outskirts of Damascus, and were getting ever closer to the city itself. I didn't know whether or not Douma was close to the airport, and therefore near the cemetery where my grandfather's brother lay, but I felt the sausages rising again in my stomach and I had to stop watching and turn to look out of the window, over the brown waves, towards the horizon. In spite of that I could still hear the reporter saying that the fighting around Homs was continuing and getting more intense, in the meantime, and day by day more and more civilians were being caught in the midst of the whole thing, losing their homes, being wounded, and being killed.

After a long time I could make out Dublin and the port of Dun Laoghaire coming into view on the horizon, and then I could see, if I narrowed my eyes, the shape of the Martello tower on the headland in Sandycove where James Joyce had lived and where he had transfused himself, in the guise of Stephen Dedalus, into his novel; I had visited the tower once, in something of a rush, after I had reached the port ridiculously early on my way back to the Eisteddfod from Connemara. There, after making sure that no-one was watching, I had stood on the parapet on the roof of the tower, had raised my imaginary shaving bowl, and had recited, in my best Buck Mulligan voice, *introibo ad altare dei*, but my voice was caught immediately by the sea breeze, and I was also by then, though I had thought earlier that I had plenty of time before the ship sailed, beginning to fret about how quickly I would be able to walk back to the port.

But it was Yeats and not Joyce that I was here in Ireland to see this time around, and I arrived not in Dun Laoghaire but in Dublin harbour, in the middle of acres of huge metal containers stacked neatly on top of one another, and this time I did succeed in finding a bus to take me away from there. I was the only person on the motionless bus for a long time, and I sat there while the radio played a noisy jig, the engine ticked over, and the driver waited outside, smoking, and then one or two rather shady-looking characters turned up from somewhere, and the driver decided finally that it was worth his while to undertake the journey. After snaking our way through tired-looking houses and past cracked pavements, we arrived at the city centre and I started walking once more, cursing my own propensity to travel with at least two bags and far too many clothes and books, past the Abbey Theatre to O'Connell Street, where it started to rain. I paused for a moment to gaze at the Post Office, promising myself, in the spirit of Easter that was in the offing, that I would return there when the rain had stopped and my shoulders were under less of a burden, and then I went on to the small guesthouse in Great George's Street where I left my bags and then crossed the road to the Long Room pub, where I remained for most of the night.

It was a bit later than I'd hoped the next morning when I stepped into the marble foyer of the National Library in Kildare Street, to claim my reader's ticket. I was led up the stairs to the large, handsome room under that dome with its blue-green coffers that reminded me of the Pantheon in Rome and which was, in my opinion, much more appealing than the famous long room in Trinity College library across the road where the hordes of visitors were led after catching a very brief glimpse, if they were lucky, of the Book of Kells. I was greatly disappointed, therefore, when I understood that the manuscripts I had ordered would not be sent to this room, for I had envisaged myself sitting at a desk under one of those lamps and had imagined that it would be a first-rate place to get a day's work done. After I received my card, I was led back down the stairs, grabbed my things quite grumpily from the locker, and was then directed down the street to some kind of back door. My disappointment deepened, then, for though this new room was perfectly pleasant, I discovered that Yeats's papers were now available on microfiche, and it was not possible for a novice researcher like me to touch and handle the real paper and ink unless I had a valid reason for doing so.

So I spent a week with my back bent trying to decipher the squiggled handwriting of the bard of Sligo in the wan light of the little screen of the microfiche reader, and it was not until the final Saturday, when the library closed at midday that I got the chance, while it was still light, to return to O'Connell Street, and scowled up at the enormous, phallic steel column that rose up to the heavens between the statue of O'Connell and the Post Office and which was known quite disdainfully by the locals as the 'Stiffy on the Liffey', before I went on to the Post Office itself. I admired its huge portico and Ionian columns from a distance for a while, taking a few photographs, and then ventured closer to seek out the famous marks left on it by the bullets, but I felt painfully self-conscious at the same time, because I had no wish to appear in the middle of the tourists like someone with a morbid fascination, an idolatrous interest in these marks, nor, God forbid, did I wish to be mistaken for a terrorist. But when I found them I was struck by how similar they were to the traces left on any ancient pillars by the passage of time, and I would never have taken them for bullet marks if I had not known that that was what they were. I ventured to set foot in the spacious entrance, still feeling as if I were trespassing, somehow, and that I should not be there, perhaps simply because I did not have a letter to post but I also felt if someone found out my real reasons for being there, they would chastise me and throw me out in an instant.

I noticed that there was a small museum at one end of the entrance hall, opening out into another small room, and I felt at last as if I had found what I was looking for. I paid my two Euros eagerly, but could not prevent myself from feeling, as I passed through the gate, that it was a little superfluous since I was the only person there at the time and possibly, I sensed, the first visitor of the day since the girl behind the counter had looked at me in a way which was as good as to ask if I was quite sure that I really did want to go in, and whether I was, perhaps, in my right mind. I understood fairly quickly after I stepped inside the reason for that look, because the museum was full of objects relating to the history of the postal service and its utterly central and essential place, according to this exhibition, in the nature and development of

Irish life. In one cabinet was offered a collection of various stamps from different periods in the history of the nation, and in another corner was a large old writing desk, dark and heavy, along with a panel that informed the visitor that the increasing need to be able to send and receive information had led to the development of the postal service in Ireland.

Then I saw an old green post box and a postman's uniform from the 1880s, and I began to warm to the place, discovering, as I looked more closely at the stamps, that the design of some of them was exceptionally artistic. One stamp in particular drew my attention; it showed a picture in pencil and watercolour of Oisín and Niamh on horseback, riding swiftly across the waves, eternally escaping. The white horse was a really handsome one, and Osian and Nia were so close together on his back that they formed almost one figure, and it was not possible to distinguish between them except by the golden wave of hair that whipped around Nia's face, for she was otherwise almost completely covered by Osian's voluminous cloak that streamed out like a tail behind them. The stallion's muzzle was pointing downwards, and his legs were fully extended, as if he were in mid-gallop, but no part of him was touching the green and blue waves of the sea, giving the impression that he was frozen there in the midst of his movement, and that the three of them were held captive, unable to return to the land of youth nor to go on in order to let Osian set foot again in the land of the Fenians, and to age in his turn. The three of them were stuck, like a stamp on a letter, eternally in the same place, in this halfway house between two worlds.

By the time I reached the far end of the exhibition, the only part which had a display about the Easter Rising of 1916, a video which showed actors reciting some of the accounts various people had given of the events of that day when the Post Office was attacked by the rebels, I had rather lost interest in the whole affair, for I had half hoped to see more detailed pictures of the Post Office as it had been, and as it was for months afterwards, a skeleton of a building with a mixture of dust and smoke rising from it. But then how much better off would I have been had I seen those pictures? And was that what accounted for the disappointment I had felt in the entrance too, when I saw the place ornately done out and freshly painted, when I had half expected to walk in from the sight of the bullet marks into the midst of the rubble and to look up and see the bare beams? I walked back to the main exhibition, and found myself inside a small hut which was furnished like the inside of a train, or to be more exact the inside of a postal carriage on a train, and the video screen on the wall was showing a film of a landscape passing by, giving the impression that we were actually speeding through the Irish countryside on our way to Dublin, to transport letters to Holyhead, or across to America perhaps.

Hearing the regular rhythm of the train on the rails in the video-window, I was in an instant back on board a train speeding towards Prague with Cynon at my side, and something better than a letter awaiting me there, for my father and sister had flown out to spend a weekend in our company.

In Koper the night before Cynon and I had spent the evening in our room in the guesthouse, a fairly luxurious place on the outskirts of town that we had been transferred to because the staff of the cheap place we had booked into had forgotten to reserve a room for us for that last night. The two of us stretched out on our comfortable beds, drinking and smoking, watching television open-mouthed until the small hours, in some kind of swoon which must have come over us at last after the attack that the cities of Europe had made upon us and all of our senses, so that we were left unable to wonder at another church or museum, nor could we enjoy tasting different dishes, nor keep on wandering through the narrow streets of medieval towns. Though I felt a pang of guilt for just lounging around on that evening, and had a dim sense that we ought to be out participating in the night life of the town, by morning the two of us felt that our desire to explore, and to see, and to experience had been renewed once more, and so, with rather painful feet, for we had been walking about the harbour and the suburban streets trying in vain to get a glimpse of Trieste past the tip of the peninsula, or even Venice in the distance through the sea mist, the two of us caught the local train back to Ljubljana at the end of the following afternoon before we caught the night train to Prague, full of a lively new sense of adventure.

I had found, ever since the days of my journey across Siberia, that the train and its regular, rhythmic movements possessed a miraculous ability to lull me to sleep, despite the hardness and restricted space of the bunk beds, and so I always looked forward to a night journey by train for quite practical reasons as well as for the feeling of romance that such a journey always tended to arouse in me. The way in which the carriage swayed slowly from side to side, like a cradle, along with the moon's sporadically bright and dim appearance, through the trees and the curtains, had often helped me to be blissfully unaware of the miles and miles of forest and plains slipping past. That night, however, when I was physically exhausted, and Cynon's heavy breathing could be heard clearly from the bunk below, my mind stayed stubbornly awake, and I just could not fall asleep. I spent hours aware of the train moving along the tracks to Prague, sometimes slowly and then getting up a head of steam once more and hurling itself forward somewhere between Slovenia, Austria, and the Czech Republic. We had left Ljubljana about seven in the evening, but I knew that we wouldn't reach Prague until long after seven in the morning, and the dawn was taking ages to break, perhaps because I knew that the reunion with my father and sister in Wenceslas Square was on the cards, and the excitement of that anticipation kept me awake on my narrow bed, so it was already getting light when I finally slipped into sleep. Soon afterwards, about an hour or two at most as far as I was able to estimate, I was woken by the *provodnitsa* who swept like a great wind through the carriage, opening doors and yelling that we had, at last, reached PRAHA.

Since it was so early Cynon and I had to wait in the common room while our room was being prepared, so I lay down on a hard bench there, with the morning sun flooding through the panes of the high windows, reminding me of an old-fashioned schoolroom, while Cynon sat beside me hugging his bag and trying to wake up and look lively, and I tried to get some more sleep before the day began again properly. In complete contrast to the night which had dragged itself along, almost before I knew it, our room was ready in no time, our bags had been dropped off and the two of us were outside in the sunshine, and after wandering around for a while, with the butterflies increasing in my stomach, I left Cynon happily cradling his pint and went in search of Wenceslas Square. I saw them from afar, standing at the top end of the square while I was at the bottom, and so I had to climb up there to them, but though I could see them it was difficult for me to take in that they were actually there at all, somehow, and that old division between my life before the journey and my life on the journey was cancelled out, even if it was only for a brief period of a couple of days, and the two worlds came together at last outside my nocturnal dreams. It was so good to see them, but it was also quite frightening, for my sister was growing up so fast into a young woman and leaving her childhood behind, and my father had already somehow gone greyer than I had expected, and looked more fragile, in an odd way, so that I was appalled to think, rather egoistically in retrospect, that I myself and my two-month absence had been partly responsible for that unexpected ageing.

But our embraces, and the shedding of worries among the three of us that came next, were enough to hinder and slow down that perception of ageing which all three of us must have shared, for they must have seen that I too had changed, and so the three of us made our way, smiling and laughing, nervously and rather tentatively at first, but soon relaxing back into our old ways, over the Vltava river towards Prague Castle and the gothic giant that was the Cathedral of St Vitus inside it. This was the centre of the old Holy Roman Empire which was nevertheless for me quite similar to dozens of other churches and castles that I had seen already, though I did feel some nervous excitement and a touch of vertigo as I climbed with my two companions to the top of one of the towers, trying to conceal that nervousness from them, as every seasoned traveller must do. But before long their enthusiasm rubbed off on me, and as I saw them enjoying and lapping up every moment of our being there in the sunshine seeing these amazing things rather than being at home in the humdrum world of work and school, I too saw these places in a new light and was able to ignore, for the moment, the limit-less hordes of tourists that milled around us, and to accept happily that that's what we three were as well, and I was even able to laugh along with the groups of men on stag weekends who were a plague on the whole city, as if they were laying siege to it, rather than being disgusted by them.

One of my favourite streets was the Golden Lane, a narrow street of little houses painted in bright colours that was as pretty as a picture. Though the street was named after the goldsmiths who used to work there during the seventeenth century, some still believed, according to the guidebook that my father had brought with him to the city, that it had been so named because it was there that King Rudolph the Second's alchemists lived, those experimenters who worked night and day to try to find a way to transform the liquids in their boiling retorts into pure gold for him, but by the nineteenth century the area had deteriorated into a slum, full of scoun-drels and prostitutes. In the 1950s the inhabitants were all evicted, and the street was restored to the way it looked, if not the condition it was actually in, in the period when Kafka lived there with his sister, during the First World War, in number 22, where he wrote most of his collection, *Ein Landarzt*. It was easy to imagine him, as he wrote the story 'Ein altes Blatt', looking out of the small window of the build-ing which by now, inevitably perhaps, is called Café

Franz Kafka, where we were now sitting, and where he would watch the poor cobbler across the road opening his shop at daybreak in order to begin his work, but finding that an impudent and uncultured gaggle of tramps and travellers from the north had filled the street and square outside, and were starting to damage and destroy the entire town, looting all the shops and turning the city into a pigsty, while the Emperor watched them from his palace but could do nothing to stop them.

Later, after a leisurely lunch of bread, sausage and cheese in a café on the banks of the Vltava, the three of us walked beneath the Powder Gate and past the *Obecní dům* before wending our way through the old town into the old Jewish quarter. As we visited the synagogue there, and the cemetery outside which was in such a tiny space, so narrow that the few thousand gravestones were all tumbling over one another, and it was said that about a hundred thousand bodies were buried there, sometimes in layers of a dozen bodies one above the other because of the restricted space, I realized that this was the first area of this type that I had visited during my whole journey through the cities of Europe, and I also realized, as I read the story in the guidebook, that it was only because Hitler had plans to turn this area into a kind of extensive museum of a race that, if he had his way, would no longer exist in a few years, that the synagogue and cemetery were still there. Here, the whole place had not been turned into a ghetto that was subsequently burnt to the ground, as had happened in so many other cities.

That evening Cynon joined us for a supper of bacon and potatoes and wine in a café on a small street off the old square in the city centre, and what with the good food and the entertaining company I was able to relax and enjoy myself more than I had done for days, perhaps weeks. I felt, somehow, with my father and sister present, that my mother and brother were also there, and we were back on a family summer holiday, and as we watched the city passing by under the lights of the Charles Bridge before we went to our beds, and the bells of the nearby tower tolling regularly, I was feeling content with my world.

The next day we had a lazy coffee before walking up and down a few streets once more, as my father and sister sought out gifts for the family back home, and then we found a place to sit on the terrace of that same café on the banks of the Vltava, and we ordered the same lunch of sausage and cheese as we'd had the day before. Unfortunately the terrace was full and only a table lacking a parasol was free, but though we were boiling hot and the sun was beating down on us, and we were blinded by the light of the sun reflected off the surface of the river, not one of us I believe wanted lunch to come to an end that afternoon, my father and sister because they had enjoyed this rare break enormously, and, luckily, had influenced me to an extent in that regard, and myself because I could not bear the thought of them disappearing, as suddenly as they had arrived, in the middle of my travels.

As we embraced and said goodbye half an hour later, back in the vicinity of the station on Wenceslas Square, I almost felt as if I wasn't really there, but was hovering above the scene, watching myself avoiding the gaze of the two of them, and confirming, without a trace of conviction in my voice, that I would see them again in a few months, and I was tempted to go back with them and drive along the A55 in the rain with the sound of Radio Cymru echoing around the car. Nevertheless I stayed, of course, but at the very moment when the two disappeared from sight and entered the maw of the metro station,

I was aware again of that growing gulf between the world I came from and the world I was now in getting even bigger, expanding and deepening with every second that ticked by. By the time I arrived back in the café on the Old Town Square Cynon already had a hearty portion of carp and chips on a plate in front of him, and a bowl of *goulash*, and was in the process of ordering his second bottle of *demi-sec*. By then I was quite ready and content to join him, though it was only just gone two in the afternoon, and yielded to the desire to drink ourselves into a state of lethargy in the dusk as the different World Cup football matches were being played on the huge screen in front of us, a screen for which I had, until then, felt hatred and contempt because of the way in which it obscured almost completely a white church and a clock with a beautiful face which stood behind it. Little of that evening has remained in my mind, apart from the fact that it was an evening of pure enjoyment, which had ended up with us in a dark jazz club, much more satisfactory than the one I had been to in Amsterdam, full of smoke and dodgy-looking characters, and plenty of wine and music. And so it was two travellers who were rather ragged in appearance and behaviour that made their way slowly, the bags on their backs almost as heavy as their heads, towards the train the next morning.

In Dublin, too, some hours after my visit to the Post Office, I wandered out of the central part of the city, through the busy, dirty streets of Temple Bar, to the river Liffey, crossed it, and then walked along the riverbank towards the Four Courts. The streets in that neighbourhood, considering that it was a Saturday night, were alarmingly quiet, but somebody who worked in the library had told me that there would be a session in a pub behind the Four Courts at about ten o'clock that night. I picked up my pint under the gaze of the curious barman, who saw at once that I was not a local, and went over to sit near the group of musicians who were already beginning to gather and were increasing in number by the minute, but I made sure I was far enough away from them to convey that my interest in them wasn't unhealthy, and sat down with my book.

My friend from the library didn't arrive until nearly midnight, by which time I'd had a drink or two, and after we'd chatted for a while I learned that he came from Belfast, and had studied in Dublin and got a job in the library in order to stay there, and that he was in danger of losing that job because he played his flute in sessions such as this one most evenings in the week, and therefore found it hard to get up in the morning. I was rather startled when I discovered all this and felt ashamed that I hadn't taken a bit of interest in him in the library, and had only asked him for this and that document, and perhaps it was in order to salve my conscience a little that I bought him a whiskey, and one for myself.

By the third whiskey I was telling him about my disappointment when I visited the Post Office that morning. He looked at me in some puzzlement, asking me what exactly I had envisaged, and I replied that I didn't really know myself, that I hadn't at all expected that too much attention would be given to the Rising there, and that I'd read the plaque in the entrance describing the fire that had been lit there in 1916. I tried to explain then how the Rebellion, and indeed the war that followed in 1919, were of great interest and even perhaps a source of envy for some Welsh people, because the same kind of revolutionary fire had never been kindled with the same passion by us. And so the place's slickness and very post-office-ness had disturbed me somehow, so that I couldn't for the life of me find Cú Chulainn or any other ghost 'stalking through the post Office', as Yeats would have it.

'What did you expect' said my friend, 'a temple? A silent, holy place where the weary traveller could find peace, and muse, and remember?' As he said this the young man didn't raise his voice, and I don't think he was angry; indeed, he uttered the words in a patient tone of voice. I got the feeling that he had been forced to explain things along the same lines to people before now, and he was fed up with it, but he didn't take his eyes off me, either, and he went on to suggest that if I had ever ventured north to Belfast I would realize how impossible it was to commemorate these things in any overt, dignified, pompous way while cars were still being set on fire and people were still being killed as they walked along the street, and while the sound of the guns of Easter 1916 were still echoing around the walls and streets of Derry. The past was too close, he said, still casting its dark shadow on today, to even start thinking about building museums and polishing plaques, 'and those bullet holes you saw today', said my friend, 'though you were surprised by how worn away they were, still seem to me to be much too clear'.

With that he finished his whiskey and went back to the musicians to join in with the next song. When I left the pub about half an hour later, my friend's eyes smiled at me from behind his flute, and the seriousness had vanished from them and the good humour had returned, and I knew that his words had been a momentary rebuke and that he had not really been angry with me, but as I walked back along the banks of the Liffey, back from the quiet of the quay and through Temple Bar where the drunks were vomiting their Guinness into the gutter and staggering their way through the gawking tourists, his words continued to weigh upon me. Under the influence of the whiskey I fell into a sleep that was alternately heavy and disturbed and I got up earlier than was necessary, packed in the grey light of dawn, and caught a taxi, this time, back to the harbour. The return crossing was a bit smoother but still fairly choppy, and I didn't dare eat another sausage that morning. By the time that Wales came into view the sea was becoming calmer and the sky was a marvellous mixture of pink and yellow and red above South Stack. As I stood out on the deck getting some fresh air and enjoying the sensation of the wind whipping across my face, I continued to feel the burden of the Irishman's words, but there was something fine, now, about that burden, because on this side of the Irish Sea it was perhaps possible for me to do something about it, and so some three quarters of an hour later, with that burden on my back, I made my way back to the car parked at the end of the headland, and drove through Anglesey on my way home.

*

During those brief few days of rest at home, I went back as usual to see my grandparents, and the three of us enjoyed ourselves eating and chatting as if I'd not been away at all. After my experiences in Dublin, however, I was determined not to let opportunities slip away any more, and so I mustered up courage one night, after the settling down to watch the news and the weather, to ask them about the war, without having much confidence in the responses I would get. But the two were in good spirits and in the mood to tell stories. My grandfather told me about the brief week he spent in Tonfannau near Tywyn, Meirioneth-shire, in the Spring of 1941. He was too young to join up himself but it was usual for groups of young lads to be sent to train as 'cadets' in order to get a taste of what army life was like for a few days. 'Goodness, we had a whale of a time', was the sentence my grandfather kept repeating periodically throughout his story, and indeed it must have been – the chance for the youngster from the Berwyn hills to go to the seaside with his friends for a week must have seemed very pleasant. Pleasant enough, evidently, for the boys to club together to organize a dance in order to raise funds to pay for their trip.

'We slept on wooden slats on the floor', said

Grandad, 'all of us around the pole in the middle of the tent with our feet pointing inwards. There was a big fellow there, a sergeant I think he was, and he used to keep his watch inside his boot, you know, and keep it by his bed as he slept, and if you wanted to know what the time was you had to find this boot in the middle of the night and shake the watch out of it without waking the sergeant, and in the morning you had to make your bed and put everything outside, folded neatly, in a little pile, and your boots on top, all polished and laced up and everything. And then what we'd do is we'd go on a march, say five miles out towards the sea and then back, and what you had there was a bunch of boys from what they called a Borstal, a school for bad boys, and of course about one mile into the march these boys would start to limp, you see, and complain, and the officers would say then, well, you'd better go back. But of course they were going back to steal our things – the rascals'.

'Another time we had to wait to go to the mess,' Grandad reminisced, 'and when we got there, the officers were already eating, and one of the Borstal youngsters went up then to make a complaint. "Sit down", this officer said, in English, as the lad went on complaining, "you sit down now" he shouted, and this boy said that he wouldn't sit down "until we've been served first." You see, you didn't go in and sit down and then reach out for the buns or whatever, no, you'd grab whatever you could get as soon as you went in through the door, or you wouldn't get a thing. Goodness, we had a whale of a time.' He talked then about one lad who stole the basins from the wash huts, and took them home in his case. 'He went to Australia later on,' said Grandad contemplatively, and Grandma butted in sharply to ask, 'He didn't take the basin with him, I hope?'

He told me then about going home to Llanfyllin, through Llangelynnin, Dolgellau, Llangadfan, and Llanfihangel, and he hadn't left his bike there because he didn't know anyone in the town at the time, and so he had to walk home to Llangedwyn, a good six miles away, late at night, and he told me that he remembered it being pitch black, but that the searchlights in Shrewsbury and Oswestry could be seen from time to time lighting up the sky, and even sometimes the road in front of him. Another time he remembered standing outside the house on the hillside, looking at the sky which was all lit up because they had been bombing the outskirts of Wrexham, which was thirty miles away. Grandma also remembered, though she lived a bit further away, seeing the searchlights as she cycled home, and she remembered the evacuees who had lived with them, and she had even been to seek them out again in the South a few times over the years, long after the war was over.

Grandad didn't remember much about his evacuees, except that they were two boys from Liverpool and that they were allowed to go home to their mother from time to time, because by that time he himself was lodging in Llanfyllin during the week because he was attending the county school. But he did remember the prisoners of war who were brought to the neighbourhood, and he said that still today he couldn't taste rice pudding without thinking of them, thinking specifically of a German who came to stay on a neighbouring farm, and the farmer finding a violin with no strings somewhere. The German became obsessed with it, cleaning and polishing the violin every night, finding some strings, and then the fun they had in the evenings and in country dances, for the German played the violin so well. There were tears in Grandad's eyes when he talked about the German going around the neighbourhood with the family to play in village halls and vestries, and about the great welcome the family had received when they visited Germany after the war. Grandad looked really proud of that welcome.

These other scraps and fragments came out all mixed together, and the two of them were finishing each other's stories, almost as if they were competing with each other, and I felt that I was back there with them, because they certainly had gone back decades. Grandma talked about her brother, Dafydd, who pretended in the camp that he could neither speak nor understand English, and so did daft things like not shutting the door behind him, or turning left on a march when everyone else was turning right. 'Perhaps he was the most sensible of us all?' 'Were you afraid?' I asked. 'Goodness me, yes, it was a strange old time, wasn't it?' was the answer, and then the two went on to talk about Lord Haw Haw broadcasting his lies and his terrifying news to frighten everyone, and some local man in his Anderson Shelter, frying bacon and listening to the wireless, and Lord Haw Haw saying 'The British are starving', and getting so angry that he ran out from the shelter, holding the frying pan up in the air and shouted to the invisible airwaves, 'Smell that then, you bugger'.

Grandma also remembered, very clearly it seemed to me, late one night when she was about sixteen or seventeen, the rest of the family already in bed and she sitting at the kitchen table doing her homework, she heard a bomb, 'whistling bombs they called them', she said, 'falling a field's distance away from our house. It wasn't our field', she said, 'it was the neighbour's farm, and no, I didn't go and look that night but heck I don't think I went to school next day, and there was a big hole as wide as this room there next morning, and the smoke still rising from it.' When I asked what one of the planes of the Luftwaffe was doing dropping bombs in the Montgomeryshire countryside, Grandad butted in again and suggested that it was one of the planes that was heading for Liverpool but that it lost its way in the blackout, 'or perhaps', said Grandad, 'it was being chased by one of our planes and they were getting rid of their load as quickly as possible so that they would be lighter and could head back for Germany straightaway.' As Grandma nodded her agreement I was mulling over that phrase 'our planes', when Grandad had been talking less than five minutes before about the German violinist, but I had to admit that I would probably have felt the same as him were I in his place. 'You don't know the half of it, do you, lad', added Grandma musingly as she turned back to the television, and Grandad reached for the remote to turn up the sound, indicating that the conversation was now over, or that it had temporarily come to a natural pause, and the three of us had landed back abruptly in a Caernarfon living room in 2012.

With the mumble of the television in the background I thought about a conversation my brother and I had had a few days before when he had happened, randomly, to refer to the odd way that we had when we were small children at school of gathering up friends in the yard when we wanted to play a game. A small group would begin by walking around the yard in a line, shoulder to shoulder, and chanting the name of the game, and whoever wanted to join would put their arms around the shoulders of the chanters, so that the line would grow until there were enough children to play the game, and my brother and I remembered, laughingly, how the bell would ring, more often than not, before anyone managed to gather enough players. I myself had completely forgotten about this ritual until my brother happened to mention it in passing, and it wasn't until then that the recollection of it came back to me, very clearly and completely, as if it had always been there.

This made me think about the stories that I had just heard from my grandparents, and I don't know if it was that their descriptions of lonely journeys along country lanes under the searchlights were uncannily similar, or the way in which Grandma, after she had described the white line that had to be painted around any car during the blackout, had failed to call to mind how the vehicle would illuminate the way, and Grandad chipped in to say that they put grilles over the headlamps of cars, at which Grandma agreed and urged him to go on, or whether it was the way in which the two of them could list effortlessly the different kinds of bombs – whistlebombs, high explosive, incendiary – or perhaps it was a combination of all these things, and the fact that I could think of a number of similar examples of their stories, which all made me wonder what kind of relation there was by now between the memories of the two of them, which had perhaps fused into one, or maybe they existed as two separate memories but they were dependent on each other and echoed each other, in stereo. If I was so dependent, after fewer than twenty years, on my brother's memory as a supplement as it were to my own memories, I tried to imagine what effect a good seventy years would have on this interrelationship. As far as I know that was when I realized, for the first time perhaps, that the two relied on each other not only practically and physically but also mentally and, possibly, spiritually too, and I could not imagine one existing without the other. As a small boy I had commented to my parents something along the lines that it was easy to tell from their appearance and behaviour that they were related to each other, assuming that the relationship between husband and wife was a blood relationship, such as that between a brother and sister or between cousins.

A few days later I found myself in the library in Bangor, with what I'd heard and seen in Dublin and in my grandparents' house still playing on my mind. It was a fine Spring day on the cusp of turning into a proper summer's day, and the roofs of Bangor glittered beneath me from my vantage point on the hill, as the sunshine poured through the panes of the old windows and gilded the beams and the magnificent bookcases under the high ceiling of the Shankland library. I had a whole table to myself and had finally, after mulling the thing over for ages, set my mind to writing John's story in the form of a novel which would, naturally, be completely faithful to his life and character, his personality, but would also perhaps incorporate some elements of fiction. Indeed this novel was a very important one to write, because for one thing it would chronicle and commemorate John's story before it was forgotten forever, and in so doing, I hoped, it would be a way of reminding the reader of the horrors of the Second World War, and of war more generally, and would show that even that most black and white of all wars was not after all so black and white, for my grandfather's brother was killed not by Nazis but by the French.

In addition to this, I felt somehow that this act of writing about him was a way of appeasing my own sense of guilt, or perhaps it was a means of carrying out a duty which I felt towards my grandfather, for my desire to pay tribute beside the grave was impossible to fulfil at this time, and that was beyond my control, and so this was my act of commemoration and my attempt to make up for that failure. I had got to the library very early in the morning, and I had sat there eager to begin writing, but I was overwhelmed immediately by moral questions. How much of what I had discovered about John's death would it be acceptable to reveal? Would my grandfather appreciate this exceptionally public attempt to chronicle John's story? The last thing I wanted to do was to hurt my grandfather in any way or embarrass him, but I managed to persuade myself that I was writing this novel as a tribute to John, and nobody apart from my grandfather, if he wanted to, need ever read it, and so I set to once more to write it with a comparatively clear conscience.

But I was faced with a difficulty when I tried to find a way of beginning the work, where should I even start, should I go from John's period in Manchester or give some background of his home as well, and it gradually dawned on me that, despite all the letters and books, and indeed despite knowing Grandad himself, I did not really have a grasp of the world and the life that I was trying to describe, and worse than that even, I didn't have the imagination to try to create it all by myself in my own mind, and I feared that, even if I had the talent, I would be committing a great wrong against John and the whole family if I tried to do that. In addition to that, some part of me recognized that this was by no means an unusual story or an heroic one, a story that would be, according to the usual criteria, worth telling. As far as I knew, there were no heroic battles, no defiant laughing at fate, involved in the conflict in Syria. It had been a mechanical, machine-like conflict, a matter of this number pitched against that number, not an account of some grand survival against the odds. John had seen some fighting, then he was killed, like hundreds and thousands of others. The regiment moved on, after they had buried their comrades, and the war carried on without them. And yet, I was convinced that this story needed to be told. But I felt somehow as if I had lost my voice, that I was hoarse, and that I therefore had to tell the story using someone else's voice, and because of that any attempt I made to start my story immediately sounded hypocritical and false. In the end it felt as if the ink in the pen had run dry, and the words simply refused to flow.

I took a break, and sat up to look around me, to watch the dust whirling in the sunbeams that moved imperceptibly slowly along the floor and the shelves, shining here on this book, and then in a few minutes on the next one, and I gazed at these rays following them upwards to where they began at the top of the stained glass windows with their coats of arms, and beyond those again to the heavily beamed ceiling and its coats of arms arranged in a neat and orderly fashion; they were signs that meant nothing to me but which must have meant something to the more scholarly and cultured students of the past, for they indicated which families and lords had lent their patronage to this university's scholarship. They were all attempts, I thought, to attain some kind of immortality, to leave their mark, and with that I got up and started browsing through the books on the shelves, taking in all the names, all the authors, who had written all these books, each one a small world in itself, each one in its own way an attempt to bring something, and someone, alive, some inevitably more successful than others, and more and more being added to them all the time. But who, I thought, ever had or ever will have the time to read them all, to weigh them up and appreciate each one in its turn and to compare them, remember them, recommend them, pass them on, and which of them would be forgotten, which would be taken off the shelves and placed, dog-eared, on the table on the way out, free to all-comers. I wondered whether there were any books that no-one had ever read, and whether that author knew, whether he or she felt in their bones that not a living soul had come to know the characters that he or she had laboured so hard to create, nobody had seen the places that they had described so artfully.

I turned the corner to the next bookcase, and saw the volumes stretching out before me, here in the depths of the Welsh section, and then got to thinking if all this was true of books in French, German, English, how much more directly so was it true of these books, with all their possible readers, let alone those who actually bothered to read, dying one by one and disappearing, and for a moment I got the impression that these shelves were slowly – so slowly that nobody noticed – being emptied of books, volume after volume disappearing, turning to dust at one's touch. What would it be like then, when there was not a single Welsh reader left? Would this grand, lovely, oppressive library be left empty, or would the librarians carry on as usual without noticing, filling the gaps with the English books that abounded in the much more uncomfortable, colder, more modern library next door?

I felt a bit dizzy after giving in to such absurd thoughts, and I returned to the table. Even there, however, I felt as if the shelves, stuffed full once more so that I'd had difficulty putting a volume back in its proper place, were weighing down on me, oppressively, as if they were in danger of falling on top of me at any moment, and in that moment I came to the realization that there was no room, and there was no justification, for a pathetic little novel by me on one of these shelves. All of a sudden I had to have some fresh air, and I felt as if I were suffocating so I got up and loosened my collar as I got my things together, but suddenly my attention was caught by a volume with a dark green cover which had not been properly put back in its place, as if it were a bit more fully grown than its peers. I felt the need to fix my gaze on solid black and white, on words, on a motionless nearby page, and so as a sort of last-ditch attempt before having to leave, I reached for the volume and sat down once more in my place. One of the librarians passed by, and I asked for a window to be opened, and felt, for the moment, a little more comfortable, just as long as I forgot about that stupid novel.

It chanced that the volume I had picked up was a collection of Saunders Lewis's essays and articles, and before long I had my nose in it as I sat at the table. What makes Saunders Lewis's essays on the medieval poets more interesting than those of many of his contemporaries, though (or perhaps because) he was not always very scrupulous about facts and depended more on his own whimsical interpretations, is his lively imagination which conveys to the reader not only the bare circumstances of the composition and creation, and a few musings on the poetry itself, but also his conception of the atmosphere and vibrancy and way of life of the period. Nowhere is this more evident, perhaps, than in his lecture on Guto'r Glyn's military career, and in his description of Guto, or rather Guto's own description of himself, one might say, channelled through Saunders, where he says that Guto was a wholly exceptional lad. 'He grew rapidly to be a tall youth, heavily built, dark-skinned, brave-faced, with a nose like a hatchet, black hair – he went bald before middle age, – hands like a blacksmith's, – was his father a blacksmith? – a champion at stone-throwing and horse-riding', according to Saunders.

The sheer pleasure of the literary critic with a vivid imagination, and of course Saunders would have challenged that definition of him as a literary critic too, but his imagination and verve are quite clear in that question which asks, just because Guto had hands like a blacksmith's, whether his father had been one. Elsewhere he is bent on representing Guto'r Glyn as one of us, someone who could quite easily be living in our day and age and cope with it perfectly well, for 'Guto'r Glyn was as strongly built as D. J. Williams, and just as strong of intellect, and he was also like

D. J. in being very fond of company, famously funny himself and prompting others to be funny likewise.' Here, Saunders's tongue is firmly in his cheek. His skill is in making and shaping Guto'r Glyn into a living character who exists not only on paper, but as a person walking in our midst, crossing the border towards us, in his words. Yes, Saunders Lewis was a creative writer, not a literary critic, for it's possible to see how he changes suddenly, in the middle of his lecture, to the present tense of the verb in one sentence, in order to convey Guto's greatness in this dramatic description:

The date is February 1440. He himself was twenty years old, I guess, and his apprenticeship has come to an end. No-one had tried to make a monk out of him. He was fluent in English. He had probably often been on trips to England as a drover on behalf of the monastery. Sheep were not the only creatures he chased; he had a reputation for chasing women too.

He landed up in Euas on one of his journeys as a wandering bard, according to Saunders, and found straight away that he had a great deal in common with his young patron there, Harri Ddu ap Gruffudd, and the two of them enjoyed themselves playing games and fooling around with women until Harri started talking about war. Saunders then goes on to describe how 'Harri Ddu said that the Duke of York had been appointed as governor in France and as the leader of the army there and that he was at present with Sir William ap Thomas in Tretower in Breconshire arranging for Sir William to become a member of his council and to come out to Normandy with a Welsh army. Harri wanted to rejoin the army, perhaps Guto would like to go with him? Guto agreed enthusiastically and the next day the two galloped on horseback to Tretower. They were enchanted, says Saunders, 'by the courtesy and welcome and by the opportunity and adventure', and then in June 1441 'the Duke of York and his army, including Sir William Thomas and his troop of Welshmen, from Portsmouth to Normandy, landed at Harfleur and went on to the capital, Rouen.'

I was suddenly struck by that name, then, for I remembered that it was from there, according to Alan Llwyd, that Hedd Wyn sent his famous letter from 'somewhere in France', and it was there that he had been on his last period of rest, after sailing from Litherland, before he marched on to the trenches. By that time Hedd Wyn, according to an undated letter from the same period, was in low spirits and heavy-hearted, but in spite of that he was delighted with the landscapes around him, in such a beautiful country despite the curse that had befallen it, he said. Specifically, the poet/letter-writer describes a strange scene that he saw, 'namely the dawn breaking far away and I caught my first glimpse of France through columns of mist'. There's something simple and lovely in that description which makes me wonder whether Hedd Wyn knew even then that he would never return to Wales. Actually, there are aspects of the letters of several writers and poets which make the reader half suspect, as he reads them, that they always had an eye on some reader apart from the recipient of the letter, some other reader, further away in time if not geographically, perhaps, and yet here the description is so quietly nostalgic that I could not but decide, in the end, that Elis Humphrey Evans had his eye fixed only on France as he saw it through the fog, taking a look over his shoulder now and then, reluctantly, perhaps, to see whether he could see Wales behind him.

And though the young Guto'r Glyn appears, in his own poems, much more of an adventurous type than Hedd Wyn, and as someone who would not care to look back, but would gaze boldly ahead at all times, perhaps it's only the nature and conventions of the poetry of the two ages that make us consider the two of them in this way, for the romantic, nostalgic poems of Hedd Wyn paint a softer picture of him than the virile, unruly self-portrait we get in Guto's poems. Perhaps Guto also took a peep over his shoulder as the sailing ship came to dry land on the beaches of Normandy during the last gasps of the Hundred Years' War? Saunders is an astute and crafty reader here too, for he notes, in relation to the fighting in Northern France between 1435 and 1450, that 'the English historians are quite reticent. You will find popular books tracing every day leading up to and immediately after the battle of Agincourt, but it's hard to find details of the years before the loss of Rouen and everything else except Calais.' That was quite similar, I thought, to the Second World War and the fact that I knew nothing about the campaign in Syria because it was the French who had killed John after all, and not the Germans, though he himself referred to them in a letter to Arthur as the 'Jerry' and perhaps believed it. After all, I thought, what kind of man would Churchill be in our collective imaginations today if Hitler had won the war?

'That was the conflict that Guto'r Glyn was getting a taste of,' says Saunders. 'He was young and in the company of young men like himself, daring, arrogant, reckless, and fighting was a dance of jubilation for them, "a great dance through Anjou and Maine" in Guto's own words.' Not unlike Saunders himself who was an officer in the First World War, and 'soon enough he got the chance to join the regiment which was under the command of Sir Mathau Goch. This redhead was a Welsh *Condottiere* in the service of England', says Saunders, 'the most famous of all the Welsh in France', and 'though they knew that England was losing, that did not affect the spirit of Mathau Goch's troops at all in 1441. Fun and games, – the English word for it is a 'lark' – that's what the war was for them, and Guto was one of them, rejoicing in the revelry.' SL suggests that it's that spirit which gives rise to Guto's rather derogatory line, but a line which is nevertheless one of the most heart-rending in Welsh poetry, which describes the soldiers as 'some flowers of war' and nothing more.

Saunders also sees the connection between this crowd of soldiers flocking to France and that other crowd who flocked there over half a millennium later. That same line of poetry, too, proves that Guto and Hedd Wyn were not that different from each other after all, because in his letter from 'Somewhere in France' Ellis Evans too describes rose bushes, and the remains of an old shell being used as a plant pot: 'a small green tree was hiding the top part of the old shell', says Hedd Wyn, 'and nine or ten little flowers to be seen among the leaves looking as heedless as ever. There's something fine for you,' says Ellis to his correspondent, 'that loveliness is stronger than war, isn't it? And that beauty survives anger; but the flowers of France will be the flowers of grief in the future', and reading that passage of his it's amazing, or perhaps not amazing at all, to think that two poets separated by almost half a millennium landed up as soldiers in the same place and linked flowers and war together in the same way, and saw the ugliness and beauty of life existing so terrifyingly close together, and saw men withering like flowers, the memory wilting like a root without nourishment.

By the time Guto visited Normandy for the second time, however, as Saunders explains, he was thirty years old and 'the English towns in Normandy were falling one by one to the French', and Rouen was under siege, and Saunders himself turns back to the present tense to try to express the agitation and panic in the little town of Caen, where the Welsh soldiers were based and the regiment from Rouen was advancing through its streets, and Guto was trying to entertain and distract the soldiers from the hopeless situation outside by composing and reciting poems. This is how Saunders then sums up those years in Guto'r Glyn's career, and it's telling, in my view, that he feels the need to refer to his own military career, saying:

> Some years ago I met a man who had been an officer at the same time as me in the South Wales Borderers during the First World War; we had not met since then. After we had chatted and reminisced and reminded each other of various things he said suddenly, 'Do you know, those were the best years of my life.' Well, that is precisely the tenor of the poems of Guto'r Glyn, the soldier and officer. The high spirits of an exceptionally strong-bodied man, full of bravery and a sense of adventure, enjoying the fighting and the killing and the burning and the myriad dangers and the gamble of it: all that, as well as a love like the love between brothers that such lively men feel, sing in his poems.

As Saunders reminds us, what is striking about Guto'r Glyn's military career is that he was fighting for England and in her name, and we read this couplet of Guto's:

Hand and eye of the lion of England,
The valiant, fierce lion of our land

not only shows this clearly but shows pride in it. That
reminded me in turn of Grandad describing the British planes as 'our planes'. But the second thing that
strikes one, in reading this account, is how different
the soldier-poet that Saunders delineates for us, that
same poet who had written poems about his beard
and boasted about his strength, or even the poet who
had made fun of his own testicles, how different he is
from the Guto who, later, when he is old and decrepit
and blind, laments that 'Tonight I am the oldest of
all', or who states in another poem that 'I praised the
edges of the world/A sweet prattle that lasted but a
moment', showing, or at least suggesting, that Wales
was part of a larger territory for him, but more impor-
tantly, perhaps, that he felt to the quick the brevity
of youth and longed to be young once more, in the
midst of his peers on the battlefield, as he wept his
ubi sunt into the darkness of Glyn-y-Groes. Guto had
not wanted this old age, for 'I've been given more
than my share', he says, 'Of peevishness or old age',
melodramatically grumpy just like Llywarch Hen,
and indeed perhaps the only thing that indicates for
us that it's the same Guto that we still have here is
his continuing willingness, even in his old age, to
make fun of himself. Otherwise the transformation
is so complete that it's not entirely surprising that
many a scholar has over the years questioned whether

there were actually two different Gutos, and that we, because of our eagerness to see the confidence of the young poet juxtaposed with the pathos of the blind and half-deaf old man, have insisted that the two were in fact one. Today, though, scholars believe that Guto changed his name, for when he went to France first in about 1437 or 1438, he was called Guto ap Siancyn. But when he returned to France in 1441 he was Guto'r Glyn, and so it's plausible to say that he changed his name sometime between those two journeys.

In due course this made me think of something that happened to me when I was about ten years old, in the third or fourth year of primary school, quite happy with my world and blissfully self-confident in the way only a ten-year-old can be. But a new boy appeared amongst us, from another school, who had exactly the same first name as me, and his middle name was only one letter different, so that the two of us were Llŷr G-yn, and his surname was Jones. As if having almost identical first names didn't create enough of a problem, so that it was necessary to use our second names to differentiate between us, his name also echoed immediately before my own every morning and afternoon when the register was called. The last straw for me, because I was already in a bit of a quandary about my place and purpose in this world as a result of this, was to find that he had his birthday just one day after mine, and later discovered that our parents had decided to take advantage of this coincidence to organize a joint birthday party for us, rather than going to the trouble of having two separate ones.

Amid the busyness of the secondary school, the scattering of pupils from our primary school, like tiny molecules, meant that the effect of this coincidence was considerably reduced, and continued to get smaller as we, who because of our names had become quite friendly with each other, began to go our own ways, choosing different subjects and making new friends among our peers. The connection was broken almost completely later when the time came for us to leave school, and I headed for university. Only a few years later, through online social networks, did I learn that he had joined the army, and had been fighting in Afghanistan, and was now living in England, not far from London, but I wasn't prepared for the shock and, I must confess, an element of disappointment which came when I found out that he had, sometime during his military career, decided to change his name, getting rid of the two first names completely, and in so doing, as I saw it, had killed off, or at least left behind in the desert a part of himself, and part of me too. I remembered then a friend of a friend who had been an experienced captain in Afghanistan, but who found it impossible to adapt to his life after returning home, and who failed to cope with remembering the atrocities that he had experienced and walked out, one day, onto the firing range in his camp in England and waited there until he was blown to pieces. This led me to think about the nature of

the return that these three men, all in their different ways, had been forced to live through, and with
which they had coped or failed to cope, in various
different ways, until I almost concluded that someone
like Guto'r Glyn, for example, would have preferred
to have been shot or stabbed and killed there on the
battlefield than suffer the shame and losses of old age.

Even if I failed quite to reach that conclusion I
turned over in my mind for a long time the way in
which the battlefield had affected these men to such
an extent that those who survived were changed,
indeed transformed utterly, feeling the need to change
their names, even. Thinking about my contemporaries, those whom I had had to help with their sums at
school, for instance, standing out in the desert and
facing dangers that I would never have been able to
face, was a source of constant unease for me, and had
led me to the belief that a man would have to be
someone different, to be not-himself, out there, and
perhaps I also understood now that that someone different would never disappear completely, even after
his return, so that it became impossible to rediscover
his original self when he came home.

It was a complete coincidence that my friend from
primary school had changed his name to J— Jones,
and therefore shared the same initial letter as Uncle
John, but I think this musing would have led me to
him in the end anyway, and to some questions about
him and his brother that I hadn't faced up to before.
By now I was increasingly dubious about my own

motivation in seeking to trace, ever more deeply and in more and more detail, John's every movement during his campaigns, and at the back of my mind there was the consciousness that I hadn't, in all the years I had known Uncle Arthur, who had fought in Indonesia and lived to tell the tale, asked him about his war experiences. Perhaps I wasn't ready to ask questions of someone who could give me answers, in case I didn't want to hear what he had to say. But now there was a suspicion lingering in my mind that the simple fact that one brother came back, and the other failed to do so, was responsible for what had developed into a burning interest in John, and for my vain attempt to get to know him across the abyss of the decades, through learning all about his background and life and final movements.

*

Two of the letters on top of the pile I got from my grandfather are in the same handwriting, and that writing is so similar to John's that at first I thought that the two letters were from him. But when I examined them more closely and took note of the date on the top one, 27 January 1945, I realized that that wasn't possible. This is a letter that was written in Burton, Derbyshire, and is addressed to my grandfather's mother. As she knew well, suggests the letter writer, he had now returned from Burma, and he adds an apology for not having written sooner, but he had been exceptionally busy. My family live in various different places, and travelling between them has been difficult because of the weather. But everything has fallen into place now, everything is ship shape, and only then does the writer feel that he can pluck up the courage to touch upon his real subject, namely that he wishes to express his sympathy for the family in their time of loss, noting that he has no doubt that many other soldiers who are now, like him, returning home are also thinking of John.

This writer too has had his troubles and he thanks Mrs Jones for her condolences when he lost his father, which made me wonder how the mother could sympathise with others in the time of her own bereavement, but then I reflected that sympathising when one is in such a situation oneself is probably easier and not harder. This man also asks forgiveness for not coming to visit her for the present because of the weather, and he sends his regards to her other son, who is still in Ceylon, before signing his name, with good wishes, B. Brindley. When I saw this I reached immediately for the regimental history that I'd got hold of a few months ago, but there was no mention of him in the entire volume, which widened the gap in my head between my connection with the regiment and the regiment as it was portrayed in the book.

The details of this letter were so different from the next one in the pile, from L/Bdr Brindley B. this time, dated 1 February, and addressed to Mr J. Morris-Jones, John's father. The same sincere condolence is expressed, of course, but this time Brindley gets straight to the point without circling the topic, describing himself as John's best friend throughout his period of service, and then he gives the raw truth.

> He sustained his wounds during an attack on Palmyra (in North Syria). In company with others of his section, he was hit during a machine-gunning attack made by enemy aircraft. Although badly wounded, he was extremely cheerful, and it was discovered that the nature of his wounds was such as to render him more or less numbed, and he felt little or no pain.

So I found out exactly where the fighting had taken place, and where he had been wounded, and I was struck also by the description of him as being cheerful, so similar to that description of Hedd Wyn in the last moments of his life. I pondered the description of his wound, too, and the suggestion that he felt no pain, and tried to decide whether that was true or simply the kind, thoughtful words of a friend who was seeking to conceal the suffering from the family. Brindley says that he died two days later, and he wished to let the family know that John had been a true friend to everyone he met, and that he, Brindley, and many other soldiers of the regiment shared the grief that the family was feeling.

I compared that description then with the later descriptions I read, the first by John's CO which was full of technical details about Fort T3 on the Tripoli Palmyra Pipe Line, and the fact that he had been taken back to the hospital at H3, or the description of the

> signalling truck upon which your son was travelling [and which] was machine gunned by a low flying Vichy plane,

and I was astonished at his ability to say such things so plainly to a grieving parent, and I wondered how thankful the father had been that he had included that detail, the Vichy plane, as if it made any difference who exactly had shot his son in the back. I had read a similar description by the author of the book I had been consulting, who used the word *strafing* to describe the attack and who noted that eight men had been killed in that attack, including John.

Though I was very grateful to Brindley for the sensitivity and tenderness of his description, and though the CO's account was valuable for its rawness, I think the simple postscript by the author of the book in his email to me was what struck me most powerfully, that cold word, *strafing*, which conjured up a picture in my mind's eye of a body splayed out on the ground, and then the shock, for someone who had, as it were, been brought up on stories of the Somme and the absurd numbers of men killed in one day, the hundreds of thousands, to hear that he was one of only eight, as if that made the whole thing somehow much worse; it was a wholly selfish feeling, as if I would have been better able to cope with it all if a hundred others had died that day alongside my grandfather's brother. Somehow this knowledge made the fact of his death seem much more real in my mind, and yet the boy, the man, remained unreachable. He was just a name despite all these details, not a flesh-and-blood person, and it was actually easier to call him my grandfather's brother, and in so doing keep him at arm's length after all.

In that essay of his on Guto'r Glyn and his military career Saunders Lewis proffers his interpretation of Guto's poetic apprenticeship, suggesting tentatively that Llywelyn ab y Moel had been an influence on him as a poet and a soldier, and may have been the one who personally taught him how to write strict metre poetry. The critic J. E. Caerwyn Williams's view of the matter is different, however, for he believes that the truth is, inevitably perhaps, 'less colourful' than Saunders Lewis's account, and he suggests that one of Guto's first poetic masters was Dafydd Cyffin, the vicar of Llangedwyn. Although the evidence to support this suggestion is quite shaky, namely that Guto called Dafydd teacher on one occasion, and the editors of the new online edition seem not to accept it, there's something in the idea which appeals to me, and that has no doubt something to do with the feeling that came over me as I drove past the wall of the church on my way into the village of

Llangedwyn, and the thrill I felt as I thought that Guto himself could have taken the first steps in his poetic career under the tutelage of the vicar here just a stone's throw from the place where my grandfather was brought up, in the 'gleaming grove of Llangedwyn', as he put it.

Indeed, I was glad of such reflections as I reached the village, for I was not in the best of moods when I got in the car to start my journey to Llangedwyn on that Saturday afternoon in April, when I hoped that visiting Canol Arren would bring me, at last, closer to John and to the person he really was. I was much later than I had intended starting out on my journey. The day was a grey one, with fog hanging low over the hills, and dew still suspended from the hedges. I think that I had looked forward, in some obscure way, to being able to recreate that golden light which was in so many of the pictures I'd seen of the place, and the realization that that would not be possible on a day such as this was frustrating. Moreover, I was coming from an easterly direction that day, from the Welsh Marches, a completely different direction from the one I was used to, which lent an unfamiliar complexion to the journey for I wasn't entirely sure where I was. It was only when the weather was exceptionally bad, making the prospect of crossing the Berwyn mountain too dangerous, that we would venture this way as a family in times gone by, and even then we would usually turn, after leaving the main road in Llynclys, first towards Carreghofa and then through there to Llanfyllin.

But on that day I was on my way to Llangedwyn, and so I kept straight on without turning off for Llanfyllin, and indeed as I penetrated deeper into Montgomeryshire, down the valley with the hills rising all around me, my spirits lifted, since I was now on my way, the fog was descending lower and lower until it almost hid the bottom of the valley. I had no precise plan in hand for when I reached Llangedwyn. To be honest I think I refused to admit even to myself that I was there to search systematically and thoroughly for Canol Arren, and the fairly imprecise plan was to stay for a while in the village centre, get out of the car and take a few pictures of the surrounding area, and since I had a vague memory that we had been able to see the house on the hilltop from the main road when we had been there years before, my intention was to take a few photographs of it from a distance, without disturbing the present owners.

As I approached the village along the winding lane, however, the trees cleared and the valley started to spread out before me, and I saw the sign for Llangedwyn, indicating that I was about to reach my destination, and informing me also that the village was twinned with Omerville. I was determined to find the exact house before nightfall. By a strange coincidence, the sign at the very next junction I came to pointed towards Mynydd-y-Briw, and my heart leapt as I realized that I was on the right track and that I might find the house within the next few minutes. I followed the road past an estate of bungalows, past the village hall car park and up a fairly steep hill that hugged the edge of a conifer plantation. There had evidently been a storm here, since branches and leaves were scattered over the road, which was getting narrower and steeper, and muddy too.

After several bends, the road forked, and I chose the track that led to the left. There was something in me, some distant memory or some instinct, that told me that the house was in that direction, and I was convinced, after clearing the trees, that the little farm would appear at any moment over the brow of the next hill. But after a good five minutes more of driving, with the road narrowing still further, a big farm came into view, and there was no indication that the road continued onwards past it. I stopped the car and waited there for some minutes, trying to discern whether this was in fact the house, after it had been transformed and developed and extended beyond all recognition, and whether the road actually did carry on past this farm, or if this was the end of the line, for now. I might still be dithering there today if a huge Land Rover had not come to meet me, and made me reverse into the muddy lane in order to let it past.

Almost without thinking, I turned the car around then and followed the Land Rover back down the hill. When I reached the fork in the road once more, I hesitated for a long time and peered in the other direction. I could see the side of one house, a fairly small one, nestling just on the edge of my field of vision, and it seemed to me that this might be the place I was looking for. But for some reason that I still can't make out even today, after gazing at it for some minutes, I put my foot on the accelerator and made my way down the hill in the wake of the Land Rover. I don't know what made me do that, whether it was fear or uncertainty, or some exaggerated sense of good manners which led me to abhor the thought of trespassing, but before I could reason with myself properly I was back down in the village. Then, by the school, I turned left onto the road that would, I knew, lead me over Bwlch y Ddâr to Llanfyllin, and which would, I was almost sure, mean that I would catch a glimpse of Sycharth on the way. I remembered that the old round cairn was on a hilltop near a small farm and yet, though I slowed down near a farm much larger than the one I remembered, there was nothing to be seen, and in next to no time the road was rising and I was climbing out of the valley towards the pass, and I knew that I was already too high up to be on the way to Sycharth, and yet peering to the left over the hedge from inside the car, I was convinced that the fields around and the lie of the land and the trees were exactly as I remembered them, almost as if the old place itself had been sliced off and torn away from where it belonged.

As I drove along the winding lane towards the pass the fog descended in earnest, concealing everything in a white sheet and preventing me, thank God, from being able to see over the precipice, for the road was becoming steeper by the minute, and then I found

myself all of a sudden on the pass through the mountain that separated Llangedwyn from Llanfyllin. The
only way of knowing that, however, was that the trees
had suddenly disappeared, and out of the fog a chapel
loomed into view, and this chapel seemed much larger
today, and had been converted into a house, and I
remembered presently that I had driven the same way
with my grandparents on our journey some years
before, and that they had told me about how they
would see each other here in the monthly meeting,
one of them having come up to the pass from one
direction, and the other from the opposite direction.

Then I was travelling downwards again and heading
through the trees and around the bends to Llanfyllin
once more. I was familiar with approaching the town
from the direction of the Berwyn mountain, and so
it was quite a strange experience to find myself on the
outskirts beside the Tabernacle chapel, the chapel that
my grandparents had faithfully attended for so many
years, and where my parents had got married, and I
felt like someone who had paid to see a play, but who
finds himself, somehow, having come in by the wrong
door, standing in the wings and being thrust into the
bright lights of the stage. But I soon got my bearings,
and I found a parking space on the main street, where
a market was held on Thursday afternoons, and beside
the old public conveniences under Pen-y-Bryn.

My footsteps slowed as I walked along the terrace,
knowing that I was getting closer to my grandparents'
old house, and then there it was in front of me, and

I felt a thrill of pleasure that the new owners had not changed the name of the house, though Grandma and Grandad had also carried it with them when they moved to Caernarfon. There was no sign of life in the house, and I looked at each of the windows in turn, the window of the front room first, the room that was kept for special occasions and where we had occasionally succeeded in persuading Grandma to let us help her light a real fire in the grate, and then immediately above that their old bedroom, where we would sneak in, before our parents were up, to eat pink wafer biscuits, Trebor mints, and to play shop. Next to that was the bedroom where my brother and I shared the double bed, more often than not, and where a picture of a squirrel eating an acorn looked down on us, or even worse, a print of the *Laughing Cavalier* by Frans Hals which I had begged Grandma to take away to the attic because I was convinced that he was looking at me, and laughing that unearthly laugh of his. That request backfired, though, because when we and our cousins were staying there at the same time, we children were all sent to the attic together, to laugh and make a racket until all hours, and with the old cavalier still smirking at us.

I looked at the attic window and then down at the front garden, which I found to be completely empty and barren, and though I knew perfectly well that there was another garden in Caernarfon which was still full of objects and figures and flowers of all kinds, it was the emptiness of that little garden that was the most heartbreaking thing about the house that day.

I tried to go behind the house to take a look at the back garden, but as far as I could see it was bare there too, but I just caught a glimpse of Grandad's little old shed which gave me a thrill of pleasure. However well I knew this place, I knew now that I would have to add it, like the house in Llangedwyn, like the letters and pictures Grandad gave me, to that list of places and objects that I couldn't approach without feeling that I was trespassing on something that didn't belong completely or wholly to me; it was as if I was fated, somehow, to be disconnected from it only by a few degrees. I turned away from the house and walked up the town, as Grandad used to say, to the other end of the terrace where the garage used to be, past the church with its red brick tower and its blue-faced clock, with the Roman numerals on it in gold, where, oddly enough, the bells were being tolled over and over that afternoon, so that the sound echoed over the town and the birds on the roofs and branches opposite were agitated and twittering like mad.

In the midst of this confusion I paused in front of a large red brick house, which was almost exactly across the road from the church and on the way back to the square. The front left hand section of the building had been turned into a chemist's shop that I'd been in occasionally with my grandparents when I was a boy, though I didn't have the same fond memories of this shop as I had of the corner shop down the street, where we also used to go and where we used to succeed, more often than not, in persuading one or the other of them to buy us some sweets or a comic or a little toy to amuse ourselves with. But from the other side of the street like this I could see that the shop constituted only a small corner of the front of the building and that the rest of the façade still retained a different and much older character, and I noticed that a small plaque had been placed next to the door frame in the centre of the façade. I crossed the road to read what was on the plaque and found that this was the Town Hall, built in the eighteenth century, where town council meetings had been held between 1775 and 1791.

To my mind more interesting, though, was the brief sentence which recorded that it was here that a number of French soldiers were imprisoned during the Napoleonic wars. This called to mind the story that Grandma used to tell me, but which I had forgotten about for years, about a young French soldier called Jacques Pierre, a soldier who I had always imagined, for some reason, as a rascal who resembled that *Laughing Cavalier*, with his wide-brimmed hat and his neat, curled moustache, and that knowing smile. The Jacques Pierre of Grandma's story was not a rascal, however, but a poor youth who had been caught up in some war and had been imprisoned in Llanfyllin, and it was only now as I read the plaque in the street that I realized that Grandma was referring to this place, and that Jacques Pierre had been one of Napoleon's soldiers. But the realization that the baroque image of the mocking cavalier was about a century before the time of the poor soldier was not enough to erase the image from my mind, and so Jacques Pierre remained a laughing cavalier in my imagination.

According to my Grandma the lieutenant was one of about a hundred and fifty prisoners brought to Llanfyllin and who would have regarded the place as a paradise in comparison with the fighting they had seen in Spain, and though the young soldier was barely twenty-five years old, and therefore about the same age as Hals's cavalier in the picture, and just a year older than my grandfather's brother when he died, he had already seen a good bit of the world. He must also have been quite well-behaved, because the soldiers were allowed to travel up to a mile from the town centre every day, as long as they were back by nine at night, and it must have been on one of these pilgrimages that Lieutenant Jacques met for the first time a young woman called Mary Williams, the rector's daughter, with whom he promptly fell in love and whom he subsequently courted, probably without the knowledge of the Rector. The latter was not at all pleased when he, inevitably in the end, found out about the clandestine relationship between his daughter and the impudent Frenchman. Immediately and in haste, Jacques was sent away from Llanfyllin and back to France, and since the Rector died in 1813, the following year, as far as he was concerned, there the lieutenant stayed for the rest of his days. But things did not turn out like that, for two brief years later Napoleon's army was on its knees in the mud of Waterloo, and the wounded lieutenant was knocking on the door of his beloved in Llanfyllin once again, and with the Rector in his grave there was no longer anything to prevent the happy union of the two lovers, a union which took them to France and which bore fruit in due course in a son, William, and a daughter, Euphrasie.

As far as is known, the couple never returned to Llanfyllin. I read later, after my interest was aroused by this story, of a visitor who came to Llanfyllin in 1908, asking to be admitted to the Council House because he had heard that there were murals there that had been painted by his great-grandfather, Jacques Pierre Augeraud. Yes, the owners were of course familiar with these murals, which covered the walls of an entire room on the top floor of their home, but what had made the man believe that his great-grandfather was the same Jacques Pierre who had painted these pictures? The visitor explained that he had in his possession some sketches of a young woman, named Mary Williams, and that they were quite skilfully done, and when he was escorted to the top floor by the owners he had been shown the murals which were exquisite and which he admired, and he in turn had shown the owners the sketches which exhibited the same skill, though naturally enough had been more hastily drawn, the three of them agreed that the young lieutenant must have been the talented artist who had painted these remarkable murals.

When I saw pictures of these paintings later there was something about them which reminded me of those fragments of fresco I had seen in San Clemente, though they were quite different in style and though they were landscapes, all painted in different, melancholy shades of green, blue, and a muted grey, and no-one could quite decide whether they had been chosen on purpose to express the homesickness and heartbreak of the artist, or whether the prisoner had only a limited palate of colours at his disposal. At any rate they are mesmerizing images, combining the naturalistic and the fantastic, representing islands or rocky headlands, each one like a mountain, with waterfalls tumbling from them into a kind of lake or reservoir or shoreline, and with an ornate ruin, like the cloister of a monastery, standing in fragmented glory in the foreground. In spite of the gushing movement of the waterfall, there is a feeling of stillness and silence, lethargy even, about the picture, a listlessness manifested in the lonely fisherman on the water's edge who seems content with his lot and who represents, one might imagine, the artist himself in an idealised world, or in his homeland, and yet all the murals exude a feeling of quiet despair, as if the artist had recognized and given in to the fact that he would never see his home or his family again. When one looks at these pictures one is almost persuaded, though one knows better having heard the end of the story, that Jacques Pierre Augeraud spent the rest of his days here in Llanfyllin and that he never again saw France from the sea coming into view through columns of mist.

As I walked back to the little square in the centre, the church bells suddenly stopped tolling, and the birdsong too soon stopped, for the first time since I reached the town that day, and the place then seemed eerily quiet. I lingered by the memorial in the square, and was surprised by how many more local lads had fallen in the Great War than in the Second, and then I turned the corner by the shop and headed up towards Ffynnon Myllin, past London House, past the empty manor house where a man went mad and hanged himself, a story which still had the power to send shivers down my spine, past the ambulance station which was built years ago by my grandfather, past the pretty little whitewashed cottage which used to be the town workhouse, and finally reached the well itself and its view over the town and down along the valley, and whose clock tower rose proudly over it all.

I couldn't see the garden of the house properly from here either, and to my great disappointment nor could I see the Lonely Tree on top of the hill opposite because of the fog which was still suspended over the place like a cobweb. When I touched my cap and took it off for a moment, I realized how wet it was, and though I couldn't feel the rain falling, the wetness was hanging over everything and adhering to every surface. I tried to imagine, from my high vantage point, where exactly the railway station used to be, that station at which my grandfather would have arrived at night before starting on his journey home on foot over Bwlch y Ddâr, and where his own father would have worked for years because he had been a railwayman. But since I had only ever seen one photograph of the station, one which revealed almost no details of the background, and gave no clue or hint as to a specific location, and since the line and the station and the train had disappeared from the valley long before I was born, I saw that I had no hope of guessing, on my own, where it had once been.

I walked down the hill again and crossed the main street going down to the river where we used to have races on the water and under the bridge using old margarine tubs, and as I walked the smell of chips from the chip shop accompanied me and I recalled our eating those cheapest and tastiest chips in the world, and then I found myself standing once more in front of the chapel that I'd passed by about an hour before. There was no sign of anyone about, and no sound except the babble of the little brook that flowed past the side of the chapel and which we had loved to visit, if only to see the Land Rover from the neighbouring farm using the brook as a drive, plunging through it and splashing water everywhere. That Super 8 film came back to my mind, with the spinsters in their hats, and the emptiness of the space where they had been was as if I had just stopped recording at that very moment, and the people had all gone their different ways after the wedding.

As I drove back over Bwlch Y Ddâr once more, the fog was even thicker, and it was difficult to see even the little chapel now, but on the other side I hoped to get another chance to find Sycharth. There was no sign of it yet, and I was reminded again of our failure as a family some years before to find the grave of

Hedd Wyn. We had been travelling through that area by chance that time, and had not intended to stay, but when my sister mentioned the place we all, almost without consulting one another, felt a desire growing stronger within us to return again, and though we did not have the usual documents with all the details and directions, my father was sure that we would be able to find the place. As we rushed through the villages the names were oddly familiar: Poperinge, Boezinge, Pilkem Ridge, Sanctuary Wood, Langemarck, Westhoek and Dixmude, but the grave remained elusive and slipped further out of reach with every wrong turning as the oppressive heat of the afternoon filled the car. My visit with Cynon was, therefore, my latest visit so far to that grave in Artillery Wood.

The best thing to have done that day in Montgomeryshire, as we had done that time by the roadside in Belgium, was to stop the car by the side of the road, get out and take a few pictures, almost as if I hoped, when I got home, that I would be able to look at the photographs on the computer and Sycharth, or Canol Arren, or both of them even, would appear before my eyes, their outlines becoming clear like an old polaroid developing in the light. As I got out of the car, I noticed that the place was silent, apart from the sound of three or four dogs barking excitedly at one another across the valley, almost as if they sensed that there was a trespasser in their midst, or that they could smell old blood that had been away far too long. I paused only long enough to take two or three pictures before hastily returning to the car and driving back the way I had come. As the valley narrowed once more that feeling of heaviness came over me again, for I realized that, however delightful it had been to walk through Llanfyllin once more, the place meant nothing to me without Grandma and Grandad and their stories and acquaintances, and the regular stops in the street to greet somebody or other or to tell a story about some place or other.

Later I found out that I had been looking in completely the wrong place for Sycharth, though I had come pretty close to Canol Arren, and yet I hadn't been bold enough, and without being able to rely on the knowledge of the place that the two of them had and confused by the twists and turns of the road, I had been utterly lost, fog or no fog. I realized again at that time something that I had realized years before on my trip with Cynon, namely that it's not the place that's important at all but the people who are there, the people who share that place with you, and that you discern the feeling and spirit and essence of the place through their memories and experiences and maps.

Perhaps it was there, in the car, as I left Llangedwyn that I realized the utter futility of what I was trying to do, and had been trying to do for months. Apart from the obvious fact that it was not going to be safe or possible for me to visit the cemetery in Damascus for months if not years, I asked myself what exactly I was planning to do even if I did find myself on Syrian soil. If I couldn't find Canol Arren on my own, what hope was there of my finding the cemetery? And even if I did find it, what would there be to see there? I had to face the strong possibility that the cemetery had by now been completely destroyed, and that I, when I read about it, when I put my finger on the letter and the number of the plot on a diagram and when I looked at photographs of neat white rows of graves, and when I read about the trees and the plants and the flowers that grew there, had been seeing in my mind's eye a place that no longer existed, and that had not existed for a long time, just as we look up at the stars every night and see them as they once were, millions and millions of years ago, before they turned into Red or White Giants, or Supernovae, or Black Holes, and that they are now nothing but the most absolute emptiness where they had once been bright light.

I was quite overcome by the absurd nature of what I'd been doing, how I had traced the history of this brother, almost obsessively, with no thought of tracing the story of the rest of the family, the story of the little sister, say, who had died of diphtheria, no thought of asking Arthur and Olwen about their experiences, or even keeping in touch with them, who had been in the land of the living until recently, and how I had been here hunting for empty houses while my grandparents were sitting contentedly in a comfortable living room in Caernarfon, where the flowers were still blossoming perfectly well in the little front and back gardens of the house. More than anything I was overwhelmed by the impossibility of it all, by the

futility of the commemoration because of the imprac-
ticability of the remembering, the act of kneeling in
front of the grave, the grave of a young man whom
I had never known except through one or two letters
and a handful of pictures. Even if I had been able to
step onto that plane, had landed on the other side and
stepped into the scorching heat of midday, and paid
through the nose for a driver to take me there, and
found, more through luck than anything else, that the
cemetery, the grave, were still there, what then? What
words would have come to me there? What could I
have done apart from laying a bunch of flowers and
saying a silent prayer that only the cypress trees would
have heard? I was not my grandfather, and if I knelt
there forever, I knew that I would feel only a sense of
utter impotence, for having failed to justify or redeem
a futile sacrifice and for having failed to live the good
life which he had been denied. I realized now that
the impossibility of kneeling by that gravestone, the
deep paralysis that prevented me from accomplishing
the thing, had disturbed me and had grown within
me, though I was not to know this at the time, ever
since the moment that my grandfather had placed that
shabby old folder in my hand.

*

I remember that there was a market hall of considerable size on the central square in Cracow, surrounded by a number of cafés and so on. I also recall

that Cynon and I were rather disappointed by the architecture, for it was quite a modern-looking city on the whole, and apart from the trams that passed by every now and then we could have been in any one of a number of European cities. On our first day there we had travelled out on one of these trams to Nowa Huta, a populous area on the eastern edge of the city which was apparently worth visiting because of the many Communist buildings that still remained standing there ever since the time of Stalin, and I'm sure that by today this concrete labyrinth of blocks of flats which wasn't, as it happened, very different from somewhere like the Barbican, would have aroused my interest. But on that particular wet day they were oppressively, greyly depressing.

If I remember anything about Cracow, it's the sounds that insist on returning to my mind rather than the sights, the sound of the trams rushing by, the sound of the invisible bell of the high tower above the square striking regularly, the mournful sound of a violin played by a small boy about nine years old dressed in period costume (though I'm not at all sure what period exactly), even the sound of the chess pieces on the little board that we had just bought in the market hall. The sound of Chopin too, for the two of us managed to get tickets to a recital of his music by a pianist called Marek Szezler. We were a bit tired after all the travelling and packing and unpacking and walking, and it was a good feeling for both of us to be able to sit there in the back row of this grand recital room, looking quite out of place in our T-shirts and shorts and jeans in the midst of the frocks and dicky bows, being transported by the chords, the doleful chords that still re-echoed in my head the following morning when the two of us started our way to the station to seek out a train for a day trip to Auschwitz while the taste of snow was, somehow, still in the air and in the drizzle although it was the beginning of June.

As the two of us stood there gazing rather uncertainly at the timetable, we were greeted by a tallish, plump, middle-aged man, with short brown hair on his head and on his grubby round face, who asked us if we were heading for Auschwitz, and whether we wanted him to take us there by car. Being long accustomed and suspicious of anyone who approached us like this in a foreign country, the two of us replied

'no thanks' curtly and then ignored him, but he per-
severed and named his price and assured us that he
would take us right up to the gates, more or less,
would wait for us and then bring us back to the city.
We walked away slowly pretending that we couldn't
hear or understand him, but all of a sudden he started
to get frustrated and angry, insisting that he was simply offering us a service, that he wasn't trying to cheat
us, and that he didn't understand why these foreign-
ers were so suspicious of someone who had been born
and bred in the city and who was trying to make
an honest living. There was a sweetness and an ear-
nestness about his sudden loss of temper which made
Cynon and myself begin to question our attitude and
feel a touch guilty, seeing his eyes pleading with us
as he gestured towards a battered old Mercedes the
colour of calf shit, parked neatly in front of the station steps.

Five minutes later the two of us were on the back
seat of the car, feeling every bump along the road
on our journey out into the Polish countryside and
to Auschwitz concentration camp, and listening,
above the rattle of the car, to Kazimierz, the affable
driver, reeling off his spiel, and to be honest I don't
think he stopped to take breath once during the
whole journey. We learned that he himself had been
named after one of the areas of Cracow, a neighbourhood founded on the old island on the river
Wisla that was known as a Jewish quarter before
the Second World War, when the place was virtually

emptied, and the inhabitants taken firstly to the ghetto in Podgórze, across the river, and later taken from there to who knows where. Apparently it was also there that most of *Schindler's List* was filmed in 1993. Kazimierz, the man, was full of interesting information about the camp at Auschwitz, about its history and specifically about the process of turning it into a museum and, in his view, almost into a kind of theme park, with its café and its gift shop and its busloads of tourists and schoolchildren, and I found myself asking him, if that was his view of the place, why he had anything to do with it at all by offering to drive people there. He turned to look over his shoulder at me, taking his glittering eyes off the road ahead for longer than I was comfortable with, and replied, 'I am crazy but I am only half crazy', before breaking out into an uproarious laugh, and Cynon and I couldn't help joining in with his infectious merriment.

Three hours later, when we were on our way back to Cracow, dear Kazimierz said not a word throughout the journey, and we two sat in stunned silence on the back seat, and even when we came to a stop in front of the station and he opened the car door for us, he simply put out his hand, his eyes lowered, to receive the money, smiled shyly at us and then returned to his spot in the station to see if any other group of travellers wanted to go to the same place, leaving Cynon and myself on the street unable to utter a word not knowing what to do next nor where to go. Even the thought of going to some café to buy a coffee or a bite to eat seemed a completely vain and futile act, which made us both feel somehow disgusted. That evening we watched the film *Amélie* on the big screen in the hostel, choosing the most cheering and sentimental story we could I think because we needed to rekindle and restore our own faith in humanity.

The following day we lazed about once more, before meeting a group of Irish and Scottish people in the hostel who invited us to go out with them to a big gay carnival in the city centre. Cynon was very suspicious and needed a great deal of persuasion, but we couldn't have been there more than an hour before I lost sight of him, and learned next morning that he'd been offered cocaine by one of the Scots, had been tempted but refused it in the end, and had then got on very friendly terms with a young Irishwoman that the lads had come across somewhere. It remains a source of astonishment to me even today how Irish or Welsh people manage to find one another when they are abroad, meeting in the most unexpected of places and discovering that they have some friend or distant relative in common, almost as if there were some sixth sense bringing these people together. I sat at the bar by myself, getting quietly drunk, until Cynon, himself drunk as a lord, came back to me from somewhere, and it was a matter of luck rather than anything else, I think, that accounted for our finding our way back to the hostel.

We found Warsaw much more satisfactory than Cracow, at least in appearance. This was the first leg of our journey, Cynon having flown out to meet me after I landed up there on my lonely journey from Moscow. When we got back to the hostel from the pub on the first night, Cynon heard slow, chanting voices from somewhere, and when we followed the direction of the music and searching through the streets we came upon a church situated rather unprepossessingly between a café and a hairdressers but which we found, as we walked through the main door, opened out like a kind of cave considerably lower than street level, its tiled floor echoing loudly as we walked across it. Midnight mass was being celebrated, and as the sacred choir repeated in four-part harmony the words *Veni, Spiritus Sancti*, the strange combination of the nocturnal litany and the Polish lager made us blush and shed a few tears, and I'm not sure even today whether that moment that we shared there, though neither of us had religious tendencies at the time, shed a kind of lustre on our time in Warsaw which could not be matched in Cracow.

The next day the two of us spent most of the day in various cafés on the square, reading books and playing cards, smoking and drinking coffee in the morning, and switching to beer quite soon after lunch. This square was much smaller than the square in Cracow with its central market, and therefore felt much more closed-in, colder, and with a tendency to cast more shadows, and yet despite this we were both agreed, after we had visited both places, that this square and the city generally had much more charm than Cracow, and that these buildings, with their tall, narrow, irregular façades and their walls painted in a variety of pastel shades, along with the horse-drawn carts that passed by from time to time, the horse-shoes echoing on the cobbles, corresponded much more closely to the idea of Poland that we'd had in our mind's eye. The McDonald's located around the corner from this main square, and which was second only to the shadow of the war in its ubiquitous presence during our journey through Europe, was the only clue, really, to what I did not discover until our last day there, and which I had not suspected for a moment while we played cards and drank at a wooden table in an ancient-looking bar on the corner of the square on that second evening, namely that this square had been bombed to smithereens during the war, literally leaving nothing behind but a heap of rubble, and that the authorities had decided, some years after the armistice, that the best thing to do both for local people and for future visitors to the city, and that the best memorial to those who had fallen, would be to rebuild the square exactly as, or as exactly as possible, it had been before the war.

The following day, our last day in the city, I had had enough of the constant sitting about and drinking and I managed with some difficulty to persuade Cynon that we would have to make an effort to see something of the city before leaving it. I had already been to the castle on the first morning, but I'd been disappointed to learn that that, too, had been rebuilt from the foundations up in the fifties, but on this last afternoon I succeeded in convincing Cynon to come with me to the Warsaw History Museum at the other end of the square. A large proportion of this museum was dedicated to the brief rebellion in Warsaw in the last years of the Second World War, and it was only by wandering around the various exhibits and looking at the heart-rending black and white photographs that I realized what I ought to have realized already, considering the flawless and immaculate nature of the square, which was like a picture, namely the extent of the destruction that was wrought in the centre of Warsaw, which had had to be recreated, this square which only a few hours earlier had been for me a beautiful example of medieval European architecture.

I read about the ghetto, and on one particular panel I came across the story of a woman called Celinka Eisenberg who was a young woman of nineteen when the war broke out. Her name now was Celina Fein, and she had moved to America in 1949 with her husband and children, but being one of a large family, she had been imprisoned during the war in the Warsaw ghetto, and had discovered at the end of it all in 1945 that her whole family, apart from her eldest brother who was living in Palestine, had been killed. It was only through enormous effort and a great deal of hiding and fleeing that she herself had survived, and one part of the story that at the time was heartbreaking for her, and yet at the same time a cause of jubilation, was that her brother, Israel, had decided, soon after they had been taken to the ghetto, to give his son, Yossi, Celinka's nephew, who was then four years old, to a Christian woman in the middle of the night, so that he would not suffer from the Nazi atrocities. Some instinct or sudden premonition must have suddenly come over Israel, because he had been overcome by a feeling that he himself would not survive to see the end of the war, and so he had said to his sister, Celinka, 'I've got a feeling that you'll survive this old war. If you do somehow manage to make it through, make sure that you go and fetch Yossi from the Christian woman.' And indeed that's exactly what happened, for Israel perished and Celinka survived, and she managed to find the woman and return Yossi to his mother after the war, when he was five years old.

Only when I left the shop and we were striding towards the nearest café to quench Cynon's increasing thirst did I remember where I had come across the name Celinka before, and therefore realized that the first letter was pronounced as 'Ch'. In his book *Five Tries for a Welshman*, which was adapted for television by S4C in the nineties and in which Huw Garmon, the actor I knew as Hedd Wyn, played the main role, John Elwyn Jones tells the story of when he was a soldier in Europe during the Second World War and the long period he spent as a prisoner of war, after a short spell of quite unsuccessful fighting at the beginning, and of his five attempts to escape, only the last one – naturally enough – being successful, bearing in mind that the rules and regulations of the army stated quite clearly that it was the duty of every soldier who was held prisoner to try to escape. I was enthralled by this series, bought the book for a pound in the Eisteddfod one year, and devoured it in one go.

I was entranced by the way this hero worked hard throughout the day under the eagle eyes of the German officers, and then every night would be either conspiring to escape, or, as he did for a while, would escape from the camp for the night to go to the nearest town to meet Celinka, a local girl with whom he had fallen in love, and her friends, and would drink *schnapps*, sing and dance and play, and make love, and then before the break of dawn would break back into the camp for another hard day's work. The volume was not without its heartbreak, because these pranks were discovered and John Elwyn was moved to another prison, where he learned after a short while that Celinka had died of tuberculosis, but somehow all this enhanced the tragic romance of the story for me as a young reader, and in any case I soon forgot about poor, blue-eyed Celinka with her blonde hair and her fragile body, as John Elwyn went on with his story making a name for himself as a renowned boxer and one of the hardest men in the whole camp. I was so besotted with the whole tale that I once dared, despite being quite a weakling at the best of times, to get into an argument with another boy on the playing field, losing my temper with him over nothing, and threatening to give him

a punch under the latch of his jaw

Strangely enough, this exact phrase, which I had learned verbatim from John Elwyn, put a stop to the fracas, for my poor opponent had absolutely no idea what I had just said to him, and so he lost interest and eventually wandered off.

I put myself in John Elwyn's shoes and imagined myself on an adventure through much of Germany, or fighting with the Polish underground against the Germans, and this dreaming did not cease for me until I read of one quite bleak period in the adventures of the prisoner of war from Anglesey, when he found himself cornered on several occasions. Indeed, at one point, while he was trying to crawl his way through a field of corn, he found himself face to face with two armed Germans who looked quite fierce.

There was a good deal of shouting and arguing, and John Elwyn was standing there with his arms up begging them not to shoot, that he was a prisoner of war and that it would be a crime to kill him, and they would not believe him, swearing that he was an escaped Jew. The matter was resolved when John Elwyn was forced to pull down his trousers, so that they could check that he wasn't circumcised, and they were then satisfied and let him go. My youthful imagination was quite troubled and disillusioned by this episode, for I realized as I read it that it would be here, in the middle of an unremarkable field in Germany, that my own personal adventure would have come to an end, if I had been a second John Elwyn, and that I would never have reached the harbour in Denmark where I would sleep with a prostitute in order to remind myself of Celinka, and then stow away on a ship sailing to Britain. More than anything reading this chapter brought it home to me with frightening clarity how much in time of war, and indeed in life, is completely down to chance. But with Celinka still ringing in my mind I made my way with Cynon to the train that night to carry on with our journey through Europe.

The day after my trip to Llangedwyn and Llanfyllin I decided to revisit the website of the War Graves Commission. I typed, as I had done dozens of times before, the surname and initials of my uncle John in the search box, selected Service: Army and War: Second World War, and scrolled down the list until I reached his name and rank, clicked on the link, and then on VIEW CERTIFICATE. A PDF document was downloaded onto my computer, a bare memorial certificate bearing his first name, rank, and surname, the date of his death and his age at that time, mottos and coats of arms, proverbs, honours, glory and all the paraphernalia of remembering and remembrance. 'In the morning and at the going down of the sun we will remember them.' 'Will we?' I was tempted to ask the piece of paper as it emerged in its colourful splendour from the printer. In those words, remember and remembrance, are embodied two actions that are better expressed, and more easily distinguished, by translating them into Welsh: *cofio*, and *coffáu*, and just as the people of Oberammergau and their *passionsspiele* had realized years ago, wasn't it necessary to remember in order to commemorate, and vice versa too, and when those who remember are gone, how can those left behind commemorate? Who is the 'we' who will be there at the going down of the sun? Hadn't we lost the whole of my grandfather's family in the past year? And who was I to shoulder this burden – a student who couldn't remember his own friends, who was not for a moment worthy of polishing the boots of his grandfather, nor those of his grandmother or their brothers and sisters, and who would come after, when the twentieth century and all its madness had slipped out of the memories of all those still alive, who then would come every daybreak and sunset to lay a wreath and stand to attention and blow the last post, and remember that one young man, a printer from deepest Montgomeryshire, had been killed, had been shot in the back in the middle of the desert in Syria, by the French, of all people? He was a lad who no longer existed except as a distant memory for one man and one woman, and nobody knew whether his gravestone was still standing, who was omitted from the history of his own regiment, buried already by something worse than soil, by layers of history which would come and suffocate each one of us, too, in our turn, and whose very name was not to be found anywhere except on a few letters in a dusty folder and on this inadequate certificate, this cheap piece of paper printed from a website, as if they knew very well that my grandfather could not make head or tail of the web, another layer that had already left him behind, a certificate that I now, at the tail end of a conversation and on my way out of the house, handed to him hesitantly and then immediately regretted doing so when I saw the realization dawning on him slowly and his lip begin to tremble, his eyes becoming tearful, and his whispered words of thanks were echoed by those of my grandmother.

Outside the house I sat in the car reliving that fleeting moment, how he had looked at the words, had gripped the edge of the paper tightly before folding it in the most tender way, then struggled to get up and went through into the chaotic study to put it away somewhere safe that nobody else would know or remember about, and I got angry, cursed the whole thing, the hopelessness of the entire business, for the first time since I first received the folder, failing utterly, just as on that very first evening, to make sense of it all. I got angry with John for going away so readily, with the French for collaborating with the Nazis, with the whole British Empire for sending innocent boys to their graves, with the Syrians for continuing to fight and shed blood and prevent me from carrying out that impossible visit, with the War Graves Commission for failing to give me anything to pass on to Grandad apart from a completely worthless, priceless piece of paper for him to fold and put away carefully. More than anything, I got angry with myself because of my utter impotence, my inability to do anything at all to ease this grief which had lived with my grandfather, and also with my grandmother, for more than half a century, and I felt absolutely useless.

Recently I had come across a news article about the current conflict in Syria, a war which had dragged on for a long time, and the number of refugees and people killed had risen to such a level that they had become just numbers now rather than the stories of individuals, and people were beginning to get used to hearing of it on the news like a kind of white noise in the background, a kind of snowfall of news indicating that nothing was expected to change any time soon, and so of course the journalists had to search around for a new angle, an alternative way of reporting on the conflict which would make people sit up and take notice once again. This was an article which acknowledged the appalling destruction and loss of life, but which put that to one side for a moment in order to consider the cultural and historical losses brought about by the war, as the bombs and battles wrought havoc on historical sites of worldwide importance.

As the author explained, Aleppo is one of the oldest cities continuously inhabited over the centuries, and Syria's location between East and West was itself of immense importance, and he went on to list the many civilizations that had fought with each other in order to gain control of this part of the world, ranging from the Egyptians, Persians, Romans, Mongols, and Ottomans to the French and British. By now, according to the author, many of these sites of immeasurable significance had been lost, the centre of Aleppo itself being a case in point, and the author tried to convey to the reader the seriousness of the situation by comparing this loss with the hypothetical complete destruction of Edinburgh or Stonehenge. Other names were also mentioned, names that had become familiar to me from my research on uncle John, places such as Damascus and the Roman fort at Palmyra, where ancient graves had been looted, and tanks were rumbling along the splendid old Roman road. Mosques, churches and age-old marketplaces lay in ruins, and it was not only bricks and mortar that had been lost there, the author explains, for it was through these places and buildings and objects that the Syrians had construed their identity, and had defined themselves as a people, and there would therefore be no hope, without this collective memory, of their being able to recover themselves after the end of the civil war.

When I read that article, my mind wandered back to my journey to Italy the year before, and to those dusty layers in the depths of San Clemente, but especially to a small shop in Venice where I had seen an ornament made of Murano glass being knocked over accidentally by a child, and then, as if I were watching a slowed-down film of it, rolling eccentrically towards the edge of the table on which it had been standing, before falling and being smashed to pieces. Even if it had been possible to gather up all the tiny pieces and have them blown into a new piece of glass, I realized that that precise ornament would never exist again, because entropy would never allow that movement from utter chaos towards beautiful order to happen. I thought then about what Erwin Schrödinger, the cat man, had written about entropy, for in his book *What is Life?*, published in 1944 after he'd given a course of lectures on the topic, Schrödinger set about tackling that apparent paradox associated with entropy: if everything tends towards chaos, how is it that living beings or entities can withstand that tendency and indeed oppose it, remaining in a highly ordered state, or creating order out of chaos, even, for very long periods of time?

Schrödinger's solution to this was that living things, through their interactive relationship to the world, feed on the order of the world around them in order to maintain and increase that order in themselves, but in the long run, and this is the key point, that they are actually increasing the chaos in the world through so doing, obeying the second law of thermodynamics, because the entropy of the system as a whole, that is, living things together with the world around them, continues to expand, and the movement towards chaos continues. In order to live, then, to exist, to keep on surviving and procreating, it is essential for us to create destruction and chaos wherever we go, and wasn't that what I myself had witnessed, all over Europe and even on my own doorstep, in my own family? In view of this, I could hardly subscribe to the belief that soldiers sacrifice their lives in order to save others, 'They gave their lives so that others might live', or Churchill's famous saying, 'Never in the field of human conflict was so much owed by so many to so few.'

And yet, I could not but feel that the price of humanity's persistent desire to live had been, lately, an exceptionally high one to pay, and I wondered whether the atrocities of the twentieth century had proved that that price will continue to rise as the entropy of the universal system continues to increase, and our need to feed on more and more chaos, just in order to sustain ourselves, gives rise to more and more chaos in the world as a result? Was not evolution itself a process of degeneration, then, as the Welsh geneticist Steve Jones once suggested, 'the perpetuation of error' in his words, with every small change, every mutation in a plant and a creature and a person, leading us to desire more and more order, and through that giving rise to the destructive chaos that was essential and which was wrought upon those around us? I couldn't stop musing on these things as I sat there in the car, feeling that I was no more than a poor shadow of my grandfather and grandmother, and of the life that the two of them had lived. But I knew, too, that that old law was absolute, that there could be no straying away from it, and that there was only one direction I could go in, whatever might happen.

I decided, therefore, to try to rid my mind of the image of the body on the back of a truck in the desert of Palmyra, and the distant roar of aeroplanes, and that disgusting word, *strafing*, to get to know John through what Grandad had to say about him, like that time when he'd mentioned that John in his day was the best fast bowler in the whole school. After my fruitless groping searches for him, trying to get to know him as he had been in uniform and in his letters and in the oppressive heat of Egypt or on board a ship, here suddenly in one brief description I saw him, tall and broad-shouldered, his cream-coloured trousers a shade darker than his white shirt, his collar open and his sleeves rolled up to his elbows, running gracefully towards the crease, stopping with his body at an angle, a little lock of hair, brylcreemed back, escaping and bouncing on his forehead, his eyes looking straight ahead, his elbow up and then his arm coming over in a perfect circle to let the ball fly, like a bullet, swinging out before dipping back in at the last moment towards the bat. I could see him there on the school playing field, and I could see him running towards Arthur who was facing him with the bat, using a telegraph pole as a stump, on a slope of the Briw mountain behind Canol Arren and having to run up the hill towards his brother, and Grandad who was still just a little lad, poor dab, sent out to the field to retrieve the ball after it had been hit for six. Or I liked to think, then, of Grandad as favoured last of the brood, the youngest by a long way of the four of them, and little Nesta already in her grave, waiting patiently by the gate for the three of them, John, Arthur and Olwen, to come home from school in the town on a Friday night to spend the weekend at home, bringing with them every time (and as a sort of guilty offering, probably, for striking my grandfather on his head once with the cricket ball) a little paper bag of sweets from Yates's shop in Llanfyllin.

But I knew that there was one letter left in the pile that I hadn't yet read, and I instinctively turned towards it as soon as I got home, almost as if to seek some consolation or escape. Only by reading them all again, and studying them more carefully this time, and trying to milk them of every hint of character or emotion, did I hope to be able to understand it all, the characters and the events. And near the bottom of that little pile of letters, fragments of envelopes and the cuttings kept together in the Christmas card, there is one letter written in ink, and the writing gets more and more round as the letter goes on. The date on it is 30.5.41, and it's full of hopes that John is in good health, and that the flies are not tormenting him, but recognizing too that being tormented by insects is better than being tormented by 'Jerry', but that he had been quiet in the skies over the homeland too, perhaps because he was waiting for the next full moon.

Hand in hand with the anxiety about not having heard from him for some time, there is an account of the small, unimportant details of the family's everyday life, exactly those details that John had been craving for from Arthur, and his mother, with a mother's instinct, knew very well to include them.

It was Whitsun, and friends were on their way to spend the weekend there, and what with them and the two evacuees they would certainly have a pretty full house. Another friend wanted to make use of the bungalow for a few days, and they would be welcome to do so as long as they were willing to live off their own rations, and then a young couple from the village were going to be married within the next fortnight. These were all just little details, but with each one the mother was spreading out her apron and reaching out her hand and offering her bosom to him across the great abyss of the sea and through the heat of the desert and was embracing the lad, her own little boy and showing him, look, life goes on, everything is still working, the routine of the world and our own little lives goes onward the same and you will come back into the middle of this ordered way of life and there will be no sea, nor abyss, nor the chaos of war nor anything else to interrupt what was here before nor what will be here in the future. And so my dear boy, it was time for her to go and post the letter down at the Post Office, and she hoped that something would happen soon so that he could come home, and though she was saying goodbye she was adding more and more details, as if she couldn't bear to let it go, but then begging God to bless him and keep him safe, she was going, and the x-shaped kisses were thrusting their way closer and closer to the edge of the page, and then an empty line at the bottom and the letter was on its way.

At the very bottom of the pile of letters, just underneath that letter, there is the front of an envelope, missing its back, and its edges are torn and mangled. On the front of this envelope is the same handwriting as in the letter, and it is stamped, with an Oswestry postmark, and the address is clearly written, John's name and rank, his number, his regiment, Middle East Forces, all in the loving hand of his mother. Then, in purple ink and in capital letters, someone has stamped on top of this address,

UNDELIVERED FOR REASON STATED
RETURN TO SENDER

and the ink in the stamp is faint and difficult to decipher. Only afterwards, after examining and reading all this, does one realize, quite suddenly, as if the envelope has just that very second been stamped in front of your eyes, that there is another mark above the address, where the edges are at their most ragged, which reads, cruel and simple,

Addressee Deceased.

and that full stop is as final as a nail.

There is one other thing among all the other trivial, important details of that letter of the end of May, 1941 which did not reach its journey's end, which is expressed in the most unadorned way, as if it were no more important or otherwise than all the other stories and fragments. Out of nowhere, at the foot of the second page, and not mentioned anywhere else in any of the letters, we learn that they had had to take somebody called I— to Denbigh the Sunday before. The little family had had to hold her down throughout the Saturday night, when she was fretting about someone called D—, imitating him reciting his chapter and verse in the chapel when he was little, in Welsh but with a bit of a twang, and then the following morning they came to take her away. From time to time in the night, she had started weeping uncontrollably, crying out repeatedly, 'John Canol Arren has gone away', but then, as they took her away, she had quietened down and become calm. The last thing they heard her saying, with a sleepy smile on her face, before the door of the vehicle closed on her, was 'John has come home'. And I couldn't stop myself playing that moment over and over again in my mind, my grandfather as a boy at the end of the lane watching the three of them coming home from school, and John Canol Arren home for the weekend once more, just like every other week.

The date of that letter, as I mentioned, was the thirtieth of May, 1941, and so it was posted a little under a month before John was wounded on June the twenty-first, and as May 2012 gave way to June and summer was upon us, I was once again, somehow, more aware than ever of those dates, having just celebrated my own twenty-fifth birthday and so having lived longer than my grandfather's brother. It was still impossible

to travel to Syria, and though I had only just celebrated my quarter century, I now had a more exact
sense of how time passed by, and so of being short
of time. When I read on the twelfth of June that the
United Nations now considered the conflict in Syria as
an actual civil war, I felt impatient, discontented and
edgy, and I became even more conscious of having little time. For some reason I am not quite sure of, my
reaction when I read this was to reach for my old travel
journal in the bottom of the drawer, and I flicked
through its pages to see where exactly Cynon and I
had been on that date, back in 2006 when we were
nineteen and the summer had finally reached Europe.

There is no entry in my journal for that exact date,
but the next day, June the thirteenth, Cynon and I
were on the point of starting for Munich, our bags on
our backs, and travelling through the countryside of
the Austrian Tyrol, which reminded me of that rainy
summer in Oberammergau. As Cynon and I jour-
neyed through Europe, on a huge variety of different trains, I started to develop a deepening obsession
with timetables. Whereas Cynon would have been
perfectly happy to relax and wander around, more or
less at random, through the continent, following his
own whims and desires, whether he wanted to sit still
on a particular day, drinking and lounging around,
or whether he wanted to go and see a church or two,
or read a book, or play a game of chess, or pick up his
pack and move on, I on the other hand had every day
and more or less constantly at least one eye on the

future, on the next leg of the journey, on knowing exactly where we were heading for, how we would get there, how much it would cost and how long it would take, and I was even determined to ensure that we had a bed in a hostel waiting for us rather than depending on fate or luck or providence and see what would be available when we got there.

I think now that the pleasure I took in train time-tables and my growing obsession with them was a way of gaining control, or of setting in order, and I was particularly besotted with the annual timeta-ble books published by the Thomas Cook company, which were a source of fascination and delight for me because of their amazing ability to set in order, and draw together, all the different times and directions and connections of the whole of Europe, stretching out over borders and territories and entire countries, in various tables which were all linked together in a miraculous way. Indeed, long before we reached Paris, I had got into the habit of copying large sections of these tables and transcribing them into my travel jour-nal, with all their names of destinations and places of departure and the different times, all precisely noted according to the twenty-four hour clock, in a manner which to my mind verged on the militaristic and the aggressive, and the gaps between the times were like a territory on a map which had to be crossed. Because of that, the two of us managed to traverse large parts of Europe with little bother and few misadventures. This came as quite a surprise to me, however, though

I didn't mention this to Cynon, for I realized that my edition of this marvellous book, which I had bought cheaply and hurriedly off the internet before we left home, was an old edition which was several years out of date. This made me feel at times that far from going on new journeys as we followed these timetables, we were retaking or tracing old journeys which had already, somehow or other, been completed but which were, in another sense, quite unfinished, as we sat there on the train living in the moment, and these journeys kept on being repeated time after time.

Despite this, I was, as I mentioned, quite astonished and indeed proud that following this outdated timetable had not yet caused us any hindrance or inconvenience in our journey, and there's something in me which makes me think that that sense of pride is in some way connected, though not directly, to that inevitable occasion when the train broke down in the station of Klaus in Austria. Not so much the breakdown itself, but the fact that we had to have a bus to take us to the next station, making us miss our connection, put a definitive end to my complacent pride making this timetable seem completely unsuitable when it came to planning the rest of the journey, so that we had to change trains a further four times, obeying the crazy and indifferent instructions of various ticket inspectors and station masters before we reached the end of our journey. But for the moment we were in Klaus, and a little annoyed at being moved from our quiet compartment, with its seats facing each other and its luggage racks above, like those train compartments we'd seen a hundred times in films, but had thought no longer existed, in which we'd sat and seen the Austrian countryside rolling past, and then when we alighted we were struck by the oppressive heat. That in itself had been a surprise because we had been tricked into thinking that it was cold outside by a combination of the air conditioning, which worked so efficiently inside the train, and the view of snow which still lay on the mountain tops all around, though it was the middle of June.

As the two of us started to sweat profusely and lowered the heavy bags from our backs, and sat drinking from a bottle of water, leaning against a pillar in this remote station, and fidgeting with the grass that had reclaimed ground between the disused lines, I couldn't help feeling frustrated that I was utterly exhausted and yet the end of our journey was still hundreds of miles away. But Cynon's enthusiasm and sense of fun was infectious, since this was the first time, he said, that he had set foot on Austrian territory, 'and if you were to dream of an ideal spot to kick your heels in, this would be it', according to my irrepressible friend. As if it were necessary to back up his words with evidence, he waved his hand lazily past the station wall in the direction of the valley which opened out in front of us and which reminded me, for a moment, of the view of Tal-y-Llyn, before the majesty of this particular scene impressed itself on my mind. The valley spread out before us as far as we could see under the scorching sun, with its clear blue river now and again opening out into glittering lakes which invited one to plunge into their depths, and then our gaze was drawn up to the hills and their patchwork of Tyrolean villages alternating with dark green forests which contrasted with the lighter green of the scene as a whole. And then even further in the distance were those peaks, pinnacles and towers of white looking down on it all, and beyond those still the sky of a blue so intense as to break your heart.

The two of us stood in silence, drinking in this view, and I venture to say quite honestly that this moment, in the whole of our ceaseless journeying, was the only moment of complete happiness and contentment for us both, a moment when we were neither looking back nor forward, nor did we have anything at all to do, and nowhere to go, and no-one to miss, but we were simply being there, regarding this scene. Such was our enchantment with the scene and so engrossed were we in it that it came as a shock, a cruel stroke of fate, to find that the bus had now arrived to take us away from there, and if it hadn't been for one helpful fellow traveller calling us and telling us to hurry up, it would certainly have gone and left us behind. In the silence that reigned over much of the rest of that journey, neither Cynon nor I could quite bring ourselves to admit that we were slightly regretful that the bus had not left without us.

When I tried to find that remarkable station on the internet recently, I was surprised to find that there were many places called Klaus in Austria, and it wasn't possible to say with any certainty in which of them our train had broken down, and so it would be quite difficult, even if I had the time and the means and indeed the desire to do so, to go back to that exact place now. Perhaps that was a blessing, for I knew that it would be impossible to recreate the precise circumstances, and weather, and view, and company, and feelings, of that lost day in Klaus station. And anyway it would be necessary to leave the place again eventually, to come home again whether by bus or by train. But if I asked Cynon tomorrow, I'm sure that his response would be the same as the one I gave myself several times, namely, that something, some indefinable element of the two of us had not returned home but was, in some obscure way, still there, still gazing at that splendid view.

PARTHIAN TRANSLATIONS

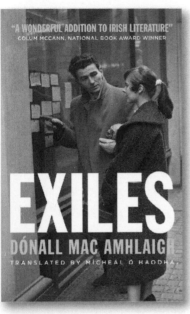

EXILES

Dónall Mac Amhlaigh

Translated from Irish
by Mícheál Ó hAodha

Out October 2020

£12.00
978-1-912681-31-0

HANA

Alena Mornštajnová

Translated from Czech
by Julia and Peter Sherwood

Out October 2020

£10.99
978-1-912681-50-1

LA BLANCHE
Maï-Do Hamisultane

Translated from French
by Suzy Ceulan Hughes

£8.99
978-1-912681-23-5

THE NIGHT CIRCUS
AND OTHER STORIES
Uršuľa Kovalyk

Translated from Slovak
by Julia and Peter Sherwood

£8.99
978-1-912681-04-4

A GLASS EYE
Miren Agur Meabe

Translated from Basque
by Amaia Gabantxo

£8.99
978-1-912109-54-8

PARTHIAN TRANSLATIONS

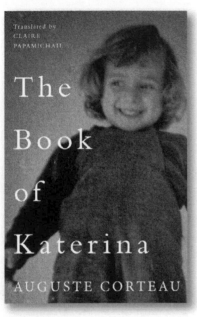

THE BOOK OF KATERINA

Auguste Corteau

Translated from Greek by Claire Papamichail

Out 2021

£10.00
978-1-912681-26-6

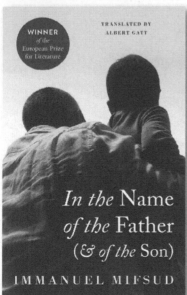

IN THE NAME OF THE FATHER (& OF THE SON)

Immanuel Mifsud

Translated from Maltese by Albert Gatt

£6.99
978-1-912681-30-3

Creative Europe

HER MOTHER'S HANDS

Karmele Jaio

Translated from Basque
by Kristin Addis

£8.99
978-1-912109-55-5

WOMEN WHO BLOW ON KNOTS

Ece Temelkuran

Translated from Turkish
by Alexander Dawe

£9.99
978-1-910901-69-4

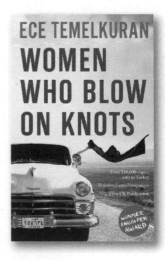

THE HOUSE OF THE DEAF MAN

Peter Krištúfek

Translated from Slovak
by Julia and Peter Sherwood

£11.99
978-1-909844-27-8

Creative
Europe

PARTHIAN TRANSLATIONS

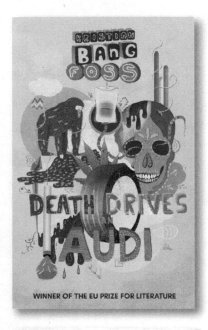

DEATH DRIVES AN AUDI

Kristian Bang Foss

Winner of the European Prize for Literature

£10.00
978-1-912681-32-7

FEAR OF BARBARIANS

Petar Adonovski

Winner of the European Prize for Literature

£9.00
978-1-913640-19-4

PARTHIAN TRANSLATIONS

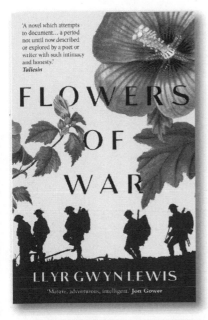

FLOWERS OF WAR

Llyr Gwyn Lewis

Short-Listed for Wales
Book of the Year

£9.00
978-1-912681-25-9

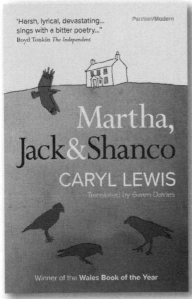

MARTHA, JACK AND SHANCO

Caryl Lewis

Winner of the Wales
Book of the Year

Out October 2020

£9.99
978-1-912681-77-8

Creative Europe